BFI Film Classics

The BFI Film Classics is a series ....oduces, interprets and celebrates landmarks of world cinema. Each volume offers an argument for the film's 'classic' status, together with discussion of its production and reception history, its place within a genre or national cinema, an account of its technical and aesthetic importance and, in many cases, the author's personal response to the film.

For a full list of titles available in the series, please visit our website: www.palgrave.com/bfi

'Magnificently concentrated examples of flowing freeform critical poetry.'
Uncut

'A formidable body of work collectively generating some fascinating insights into the evolution of cinema.'
Times Higher Education Supplement

'The series is a landmark in film criticism.'
Quarterly Review of Film and Video

Xiao Wu · Platform · Unknown Pleasures

Jia Zhangke's 'Hometown Trilogy'

Michael Berry

A BFI book published by Palgrave Macmillan

First published in 2009 by
PALGRAVE MACMILLAN

on behalf of the

BRITISH FILM INSTITUTE
21 Stephen Street, London W1T 1LN
<www.bfi.org.uk>

There's more to discover about film and television through the BFI. Our world-renowned archive, cinemas, festivals, films, publications and learning resources are here to inspire you.

Palgrave Macmillan in the UK is an imprint of Macmillan Publishers Limited, registered in England, company number 785998, of Houndmills, Basingstoke, Hampshire RG21 6XS. Palgrave Macmillan in the US is a division of St Martin's Press LLC, 175 Fifth Avenue, New York, NY 10010. Palgrave Macmillan is the global academic imprint of the above companies and has companies and representatives throughout the world. Palgrave® and Macmillan® are registered trademarks in the United States, the United Kingdom, Europe and other countries.

Series cover design: Ashley Western
Series text design: ketchup/SE14
Images from *Xiao Shan Going Home*, Beijing Film Academy; *La condition canine*, Jia Zhangke; *Xiao Wu*, © Radiant Advertising Company/Hu Tong Communications; *The True Story of Ah Q*, China Film Export & Import Corporation; *Platform*, © Hu Tong Communications/© T-Mark; *Unknown Pleasures*, © Office Kitano/ © Lumen Film/© E Pictures; *Still Life*, © Xstream Pictures Ltd; *The World*, © Office Kitano/© Lumen Films/ © Xstream Pictures Ltd.

Set by Cambrian Typesetters, Camberley, Surrey
Printed in China

This book is printed on paper suitable for recycling and made from fully managed and sustained forest sources. Logging, pulping and manufacturing processes are expected to conform to the environmental regulations of the country of origin.

British Library Cataloguing-in-Publication Data
A catalogue record for this book is available from the British Library

ISBN 978–1–84457–262–5

Contents

Acknowledgments

Thanks to Jia Zhangke for inspiring this project with his beautiful films. I thank Rebecca Barden from the British Film Institute for her patience and support of this book. I am also indebted to the rich body of scholarship that has appeared in recent years on Jia Zhangke and his films. Special thanks to Mingwei Song, Weijie Song, Xiaojue Wang and the two anonymous readers who graciously agreed to read the manuscript and offer valuable input and suggestions. Thanks to David Der-wei Wang, Kent Jones, Edward Gunn, Richard Peña, Lee Min, Chris Berry, Chow Keung and Nelson Yu Lik-Wai for their input and generosity. The University of California, Santa Barbara, provided me with a teaching leave to complete work on this project. I appreciate the editorial and design contributions of Joy Tucker and Sophia Contento. From its earliest inception to the final draft, Suk-Young Kim has been beside me to offer her insight and support for which I am grateful. The trilogy is, in many ways, about the search for family and that place we call home; I dedicate this book to my parents Beverly and Mac St John, John and Abby Berry, and my brother John, who have always provided that place I can come back to.

A note on romanisation
All Chinese names and titles are rendered according to the standard *pinyin* system, thus Jia Zhangke is used instead of Jia Zhang-ke, Jia Zhang Ke or Zhang Ke Jia, as the director is sometimes alternately credited. Exceptions include proper names in which the individual is known by a Cantonese or anglicised form, for example, cinematographer Nelson Yu Lik Wai, whose name would otherwise be rendered Yu Liwei in *pinyin* (the *pinyin* romanisation for such names is provided in parenthesis in the Credits section).

Preface

Like many local Chinese audiences in the late 1990s, I was first introduced to the work of Jia Zhangke through a series of low-quality bootleg recordings. These recordings were burned onto VCDs, video compact discs, that were extremely popular in China in the years leading up to the widespread introduction of DVDs. Unlike most VCDs, which usually came in plastic jewel cases similar to standard dual-disc CD cases, Jia's films usually came in thin brown paper bags – and they weren't out on the shelf. You had to ask for them at one of the few 'hip' video stores in cities like Beijing and Shanghai that carried such pop-culture contraband. For most Chinese audiences, those bootleg VCDs in the little brown paper bags sold at shady video stores throughout China's cities were the *only way* they could see the films of Jia Zhangke, or the work of his contemporaries, at least the more edgy ones.[1] In the west, however, the market for Jia's films was very different.

Outside of China, Jia's screening room was not the bedrooms and living rooms of film fans and students, but the glorious halls of the international film festivals of Venice, Cannes, Tokyo and New York. It was at the 40th New York Film Festival that I first met Jia Zhangke. Jia was in town with his producer and editor Chow Keung to screen *Unknown Pleasures* (*Ren xiaoyao*) (2002) and I was his interpreter, a side-job I had occasionally taken on while a doctoral student at Columbia. It was in the green room at Alice Tully Hall after one of the film's screenings that critic Kent Jones tapped Jia on the shoulder and announced, 'Marty wants to meet you . . .' and turning to me, 'Can you come and interpret?' We ended up meeting Martin Scorsese at his mid-town office, and almost instantaneously, Scorsese, speaking at break-neck speed, began describing in his trademark New York accent how he had first come to hear about and subsequently see Jia's feature-length debut, *Xiao Wu* (1997). He talked about circling the description of the film in a festival catalogue several years before when it originally perked his interest, and how he finally screened it alone on video while in Italy shooting *Gangs of New York* (2002). Brimming with enthusiasm, Scorsese described several of his favourite scenes from the film to a thirty-two-year-old Jia, who sat quietly, before going on to compare the energy and vision of the film to his own early masterpiece, *Mean Streets* (1973). 'Every ten, twenty, thirty years, someone comes along and they reinvent cinema . . .' the fevered intensity of Scorsese's voice increased, 'You reinvented cinema.'[2]

Two years later, I taught *Xiao Wu* in a university course on Contemporary Chinese Fiction and Film. As the lights came up after our classroom screening, I scanned the room looking for signs that the students had been as blown away by the film as Scorsese, or any number of other critics or film fans, myself included, that had been utterly floored by the film's sheer passion, honesty and power – there were few. The typical reaction seemed to be more akin to, 'Why did you make us watch that?' 'What was the point of that film?' 'It just felt like some Chinese home movie' or more simply, 'Boring . . .'. Apparently, reinventing cinema is relative.

A similar disparity can also be seen in the film's reception at home and abroad. Of course, such a disparity in reactions could easily be boiled down to the longstanding rift between art cinema and commercial film. But in the case of *Xiao Wu* this dichotomy is further complicated when we look at the film's dramatically different reception in China and in international markets, which also ties into the western appetite for films 'banned in China' and the Chinese aversion to films construed as having hung out – if not waved – their dirty laundry to the world. Yingjin Zhang has astutely summarised different receptions to the film in different markets:

After winning a top prize at the 1997 Berlin film festival, [*Xiao Wu*] picked up distributors in France, Germany, Belgium, Switzerland, Austria, Australia,

Japan, South Korea, and Hong Kong. In January 1999, the film showed in four French theaters and reportedly topped the French box office for four weeks . . . In sharp contrast, a few film screenings in Beijing in 1998 generated mixed but mostly negative responses . . . The first one at Beijing University was hosted by the poet Xie Mian and attended by thirty or so faculty members, but one of them criticized the film for describing China as a poverty-stricken third-world country. Xie Fei, a professor and film director at the Beijing Film Academy . . . arranged a clandestine screening on the academy's campus, after which the film went on to be ridiculed as a negative example in some class lectures.[3]

The response to *Xiao Wu* in China has greatly changed in the decade since those early screenings, with many Chinese film critics now regarding the film as a milestone in the history of Chinese cinema.[4] But those initial reactions during those 1998 screenings in Beijing still stand as a powerful testament to radically different responses *Xiao Wu* has inspired among different viewers.

This extreme exercise in audience response speaks powerfully to the ways in which audiences create their own meaning from the images on the screen, but also attests to the complexity of the original text. Films like *Xiao Wu*, *Platform* (*Zhantai*) (2000) and *Unknown Pleasures* may play to some mainstream audiences as a series of amateur cinematic exercises lacking in tension, plot development and drama; however, those who dig just a bit deeper will find that hidden beneath that surface is a rich nuanced world laden with passion, power, sensitivity to detail and a meticulously designed narrative arc. The ability to bridge these two poles is part of what makes Jia's work as a film-maker so special. Jia's early work consists of a series of low-budget films employing non-professional actors about everyday life in small-town China; while the subject matter and presentation may appear crude, they are portraits drawn with masterful visual strokes, displaying sensitivity, style and more than their fair share of cinematic brilliance. To weave stories that contain all the drama and tragedy of *King Lear* yet unfold so naturally that some audiences mistake them for 'some Chinese home movie' or even 'a negative example' of film-making – that is the true genius of Jia Zhangke. This book marks an attempt to move beyond the unassuming façade of Jia's work and reveal a carefully designed cinematic universe that has provided one of the most powerful and poignant sets of screen memories for our time.

1 Prelude: Trying to Get Back Home

Jia Zhangke's personal hometown – and the cinematic hometown of his first two feature-length films – is Fenyang, a small city on the westerly side of central Shanxi province. Known for its production of local spirits and famous for the several legendary generals that hailed from Fenyang, the area is also surrounded by coalmines, which are a major part of the local economy. Jia was born in this small county town in May 1970; his father was a Chinese-language teacher and his mother was a sales clerk. He had a somewhat rebellious childhood in Fenyang where he performed poorly in school and befriended a group of hoodlums that became his 'sworn brothers'. The sweeping economic reforms that transformed China's urban centres in the 1980s may not have had as an immediate and visible impact on smaller cities like Fenyang, but even there the effects gradually trickled down. By the age of twenty, Jia Zhangke was yearning for an opportunity to see the outside world and went to the provincial seat of Taiyuan some 108 kilometres away. In Taiyuan Jia studied art at Shanxi University; however, as the director later recounted, it was not necessarily his artistic ideals that originally drove him:

If I ever wanted to live in another city there were only two options, joining the army or getting into college. Joining the army would have been an impossibility for me, which left college as the only option. But because my grades in school were so poor, I went to study painting since the academic requirements at the art institute were relatively lax – all the kids who flocked to college to major in art were thinking the same thing. At that time we didn't have dreams or ideals, all we wanted was to survive.[5]

It was during his time as an art student at Shanxi University that Jia Zhangke first discovered the power of cinema when he happened to wander into a theatre screening a print of *Yellow Earth* (*Huang tudi*) (1984), Chen Kaige's influential film about a communist soldier who travels to a remote village in Shaanxi to collect local folk songs. The setting of the film, which bore similarities to the world in which Jia grew up, instantly struck him, as did the film's powerful visual style. As Jia would later recall, '[At the time,] I didn't have the slightest notion who Chen Kaige was or what *Yellow Earth* was about. But that film changed my life. It was at that moment, after watching *Yellow Earth*, that I decided I wanted to become a director and my passion for film was born.'[6] That cinematic epiphany led Jia to apply to film school and in 1993, at the age of twenty-three, Jia was admitted to the prestigious Beijing Film Academy. Jia applied to the literature department (which was essentially a film-theory emphasis) in order to avoid the fierce competition to be admitted to the film-directing major. But the aspiring director quickly created his own opportunities to gain experience behind the camera. It was during his sophomore year in Beijing that Jia, along with a group of his classmates, formed a film club in order to produce their own student films. Inspired by the first wave of independent Chinese film-makers like Zhang Yuan, Wang Xiaoshuai and Wu Wenguang who had emerged just a few years earlier, the Practical Film Group worked together on the production of several short student film projects. It wasn't long before Jia directed his first short with the group, *One Day in Beijing* (*You yi tian, zai Beijing*) (1994), a video portrait of tourists in Tiananmen Square shot on Betacam. As an outsider, then in Beijing for only one year, the short can be seen as Jia's opportunity to reflect on the pilgrimage so many Chinese from the provinces make to the physical and political heart of China, Tiananmen Square in Beijing. Jia's camera captures a curious melding of the most mundane of activities carried out at a site forever linked with the epic.

The following year Jia directed a much more substantial short that would mark the formation of his signature aesthetic style as well as many of the central themes he would continue to explore in his

Wang Hongwei as
Xiao Shan in *Xiao Shan
Going Home*

early feature-length films. *Xiao Shan Going Home* (*Xiao Shan hui jia*) (1995) traces a few days in the life of a migrant worker in Beijing. As the Chinese New Year draws near, Xiao Shan, an out-of-work restaurant cook, decides to return home to visit his family for the holiday. The entire fifty-eight-minute film traces Xiao Shan's journey – not as he returns home – but as he traverses Beijing calling on a variety of characters including a university student, a ticket scalper and a prostitute in hopes of finding someone to accompany him back to his hometown.

In the end, however, all of Xiao Shan's hometown friends have elected to stay in Beijing for the holiday and he fails to find a travel companion to accompany him back to Henan. Xiao Shan abandons his trip and the film concludes with the symbolic gesture of Xiao Shan having his long hair cut.

The unavailability and disinterest expressed by Xiao Shan's old friends at the prospect of returning home points to a new social order. Most of Xiao Shan's friends stay behind in order to work and earn extra money over the holiday, signalling a shift from traditional family values to new economic values. In this new social order, the lunar New Year – traditionally the most important Chinese holiday where families celebrate together while businesses and commercial life shut down – has been sacrificed to fuel China's economic engine.

The loss of this traditional hometown return and family reunion takes on an even more ironic tone by positioning Anyang as the site of Xiao Shan's hometown. Anyang, which lies in northern Henan province, is not a typical small town, but generally regarded as one of the cradles of early Chinese civilisation. Home to numerous archaeological sites dating as far back as to the Stone Age when the area around the city was occupied by cave people, Anyang was also the site of the first capital city in Chinese history during the Shang dynasty (1766–1050 BC). Anyang's rich history thus positions the city not just as Xiao Shan's hometown, but the ontological hometown of the Chinese people. When Xiao Shan and his friends each decide to forgo their trip home, Jia is presenting a powerful critique about what is lost along the marathon route to modernisation.

In the absence of a physical return to the hometown of Anyang – or Fenyang – lies a deep psychological nostalgia and it is this unrequited yearning that is the true subject of Jia's film. *Xiao Shan Going Home* is not about *going* home, but, rather, *longing* for home. It is precisely this common longing that brings Xiao Shan together with such a disparate array of characters from different walks of life, socials classes and professions; binding them together is their common spoken dialect, local culture, hometown memories and collective exile. This was also a subject intimately close to Jia Zhangke, who himself had seldom returned to his own hometown of Fenyang since arriving in Beijing. But Jia would make his cinematic return to his home province of Shanxi where he would shoot his first three feature-length productions – *Xiao Wu*, *Platform* and *Unknown Pleasures* – which together are the focus of this study. The three films form a trilogy not in the sense of any true narrative continuity between the stories or characters, but rather in terms of their shared aesthetic vision, social critique and, certainly, the common socio-geographic-historic terrain trough which they traverse.[7]

On several levels, Jia's trilogy challenges the notion of the 'hometown' or *guxiang* as it has been represented over the long course of China's history. In early Chinese literature, the hometown was often the object of longing, written about by scholars, poets and literati while fulfilling court duties far away from home, in exile, or in retreat from the affairs of the world. For these individuals the hometown became an idyllic, often idealised, site upon which to project one's hopes and nostalgia. Perhaps the most famous example is the Tang poet Li Bai's short poem, 'Quiet Night' ('Jing je', also 'Jing ye si').

> The moon shines brightly on the floor before my bed
> It appears like frost coating the floor
> I raise my head to gaze at the moon
> I lower my head and think of my old home.

The poem is not only regarded as one of the masterpieces of Chinese poetry, it is also the first poem most Chinese children learn in school. This presentation of the hometown as an idealised site one dreams of on moonlit nights is thus one that remains indelibly etched on the Chinese psyche. In the modern era as China found itself caught in a century of turmoil and transformation, the concept of an imagined hometown where everything remained untouched by the calamities outside would continue as a source of consolation for many. In 1921, Lu Xun, the father of modern Chinese fiction published one of his most celebrated short stories, 'My Old Home' ('Guxiang'). In the story, the narrator returns to his hometown after twenty years only to be struck by a visceral disconnect between the idealised memories of his childhood there and the depressing reality of his home's current state. And though the *guxiang* was already beginning to transform, from Li Bai to Lu Xun, literary imaginations of the hometown have almost always been framed with a melancholic longing and projected from a site far removed.

Numerous critics have all emphasised the central place of the 'native home' or 'hometown' in Jia's films. Jonathan Rosenbaum has noted, 'the fact that he hails from the small town of Fenyang in northern China's Shanxi province clearly plays an important role in all his features to date', and Kevin Lee has written, 'By looking at Jia's films, all set in Shanxi, one perceives that his rural upbringing has had a profound effect on his aesthetic.'[8] But in many ways, Jia offers a very different approach to the hometown than has been imagined in earlier literary and cinematic texts. Set primarily in Shanxi, the spatial distance that framed earlier visions of the *guxiang* (including Jia's own *Xiao Shan Going Home*) is largely removed, as are the nostalgic yearnings that often accompany that distance. And unlike Lu Xun's story where time and the distortion of memory has gradually rendered the hometown a strange, unrecognisable place, in Jia's work we see the hometown eroding before our very eyes. What we witness is an *implosion* of the hometown as relationships, moral codes, ways of life and even physical structures are disassembled and destabilised before the protagonists can even comprehend the changes, let alone regain their bearings. With the deterioration of old communist ideals and the onslaught of global capitalism, the hometown of Jia's trilogy is in a state of constant flux. As Li Tuo has noted, although the representations of hometown life in his films appear 'stable, on one level you could even say it exists in a state of stagnation. At the same time it is in the process of being destroyed and shattered amid the process of modernization. However . . . Jia Zhangke has discovered a certain poeticism amid this stagnation and destruction.'[9]

More so than any other film-maker of his generation, Jia has cinematically embraced his hometown, repeatedly returning there to breathe new cinematic life into his ever-expanding cinematic canvas. Jia's trilogy forgoes a vision of the hometown as the idyllic countryside (or later conceptions of the hometown as the Olympian metropolis) in favour of Fenyang – small-town China. Breaking the dichotomy between the city and the country, setting his films in Shanxi, located on the cusp of the urban and rural, effectively creates a new vision of where the 'hometown' lies. In this sense, Fenyang and the other sites of Jia's films can be seen as a conscious attempt to

remap small-town China as the true heart of the country.
The hometown is not just home to the protagonists; on one level, it
serves as the ontological hometown of all of China.[10]
Like Yoknapatawpha County in the fiction of Faulkner or Northeast
Gaomi County in the novels of Mo Yan, through Jia's films – and
sometimes the films of his collaborators Yu Lik Wai and Han Jie –
Fenyang county (or more broadly Shanxi province) has emerged a
key site for imagining representing and reimagining small-town
China and the Chinese 'everyman'. Continually returning to the same
small-town location to build up a entire corpus of works is a feat
seldom attempted in the history of cinema. With cities, of course, it is
much more common; think Almodóvar's Madrid, Fellini's Rome, or
Edward Yang's Taipei, but Jia's experiment is much more bold in the
sense that he has taken an essentially unknown backwater like
Fenyang and transformed it into a site emblematic of all of China.[11]

Further uniting Jia Zhangke's first three features is also their
common independent spirit and status as 'underground' films, which
denied them theatrical release in China. (Jia's underground status
would change for his fourth feature, *The World* [*Shijie*] [2004],
which was produced by the Shanghai Film Studio and was the
director's first film to be commercially released in China.) The trilogy
also highlights Jia's collaborative relationship with a key group of
film-makers, including cinematographer Yu Lik Wai, producer Li Kit-
Ming, producer/editor Chow Keung and actors such as Wang
Hongwei and Zhao Tao. At the same time, each film presents an
important stage in the evolution of Jia Zhangke's cinematic
development, as evidenced even by the chosen form – 16mm (*Xiao
Wu*), 35mm (*Platform*) and Digital (*Unknown Pleasures*) – as well as
an increasingly transnational production model, which took Jia from
Beijing (*Xiao Wu*) to Hong Kong (*Platform*) and, ultimately, to
France (*Unknown Pleasures*) for development, processing and post-
production.

Throughout his career, Jia has positioned himself as
uncompromisingly independent. This identity can be seen

throughout Jia Zhangke's corpus of cinematic work that eschews commercial modes of film-making for a fiercely independent vision that includes non-professional actors, extended takes, unconventional narrative structures and even extended film run times. Jia has reflected on his often precarious status as an independent film-maker in his actual work. This was the case in 2001 when Jia directed *La condition canine* (*Gou de zhuangtai*), a short five-minute film documenting a group of puppies being sold at a market in China.

The film portrayed a group of dogs tied up together in a burlap sack as the slowly panning camera patiently follows the movements of the squirming animals inside. Gradually, a single dog manages to wedge its snout through a tiny hole in the bag and, pushing its nose further, the puppy is able to squeeze its entire head through the hole and gasp for air. Jia used the short film to comment on the suffocating nature of independent cinema in China and provide a powerful statement about just how difficult it is for artists to breath when working within a system that censors, restricts creativity and lacks the infrastructure to support independent arts. This extremely self-conscious positioning of himself as an 'independent artist', or perhaps even 'endangered species', is displayed not only through

Breaking free: *La condition canine*

Jia's allegorical cinematic gestures, such as *La condition canine*, but also more blatantly through public discourse.

This independent sensibility is also evidenced by a strong tension between Jia's oeuvre and the cinematic spirit represented by the Fifth Generation, the first post-Cultural Revolution class of film-makers to graduate from the Beijing Film Academy in 1982. While *Yellow Earth*, one of the early cornerstone films of the Fifth Generation still stands as one of Jia's key influences, as Chen Kaige, Zhang Yimou and other Fifth Generation film-makers gravitated increasingly towards big-budget fantasy epics and historical costume dramas, the strong ideological and aesthetic rift between their work and Jia's own cinematic direction became increasingly evident. Often described as a member of the 'Sixth Generation', Jia's cinematic approach eschews the temptations of melodrama, fantasy, comedy and other commercial forms in favour of a realist aesthetic that highlights the plight of the everyman. Jia's generation of film-makers also began to turn away from the literary sources upon which so many of the Fifth Generation directors had established their careers – *Red Sorghum* (*Hong gaoliang*) (1987), *Ju Dou* (1990), *Farewell My Concubine* (*Bawang bieji*) (1993), *To Live* (*Huozhe*) (1994) and most of the other best-known films of the Fifth Generation were adaptations from works of Chinese fiction – in favour of shooting stories inspired by real life which often reflected a highly personal dimension (although in the section on *Xiao Wu* I argue that the Sixth Generation break with revolutionary literary sources may not be as thorough as one might assume).

Critics Wang Hui and Jason McGrath have both astutely identified two primary aesthetic models that inform Jia's work, the post-1990s post-socialist realism movement in Chinese film (especially documentaries) and international art cinema (with special emphasis on the work of Hou Hsiao-hsien and Ozu Yasujiro).[12] It would be these influences combined with the experience of growing up in the new media age of the reform era, as well as a resilient attachment to his native home that would help shape Jia's unique cinematic world. As the Fifth Generation gravitated towards the 'Hollywood blockbuster' model in the 2000s, the tension between their glossy 'made-for-metroplex' imagined past and Jia Zhangke's gritty vision of contemporary reality became increasingly clear. This tension transformed into antagonism in 2006 when Jia decided to release his award-winning art film *Still Life* (*Sanxia haoren*) (2006) the same day as Zhang Yimou's pan-Chinese martial arts extravaganza *Curse of the Golden Flower* (*Mancheng jindai huangjinjia*) (2006). Jia added fuel to the fire by launching a series of public attacks on the veteran director's artistic failure in the face of commercial temptation.[13] Such engagement is another means of Jia further positioning himself as the 'puppy breaking out of the canvas sack'. One, however, cannot overlook the blatant ways in which engaging in such a public criticism and choosing to release his film the same day as *Curse* is also fuelled by its own set of commercial desires. And while Jia has been remarkably loyal to his artistic ideals, even after going above-ground to make films in concert with state-approved studios, even he is not immune from the temptations of commercialism, a fact best evidenced by a 2007 short film he directed for the Ford Motor Company along with other television commercials he helmed for such companies as Olay.

Produced between 1997 and 2002, Jia's 'Hometown Trilogy' represents the first phase of Jia's career as a truly 'underground film-maker'. The trilogy is set in the director's home province of Shanxi and each instalment highlights the plight of marginalised individuals – singers, dancers, pickpockets, prostitutes and drifters – as they struggle to navigate through the radically transforming terrain of contemporary China. *Xiao Wu* is the story of a small-time pickpocket who faces the breakdown of his relationships with his friends, family and girlfriend amid a local crackdown on crime, which Xiao Wu ultimately falls victim to. *Platform*, often considered Jia's most ambitious film, is an epic narrative that bears witness to China's roaring 1980s and the radical transformation from socialism to capitalism. Spanning ten years in the life of a Shanxi-based song and dance troupe, *Platform* offers a sophisticated and penetrating cinematic poem about time, change and coming of age. Because of its important place in modern Chinese cinema, the longest and most detailed section in this current book is also devoted to *Platform*.

Jia's third feature, *Unknown Pleasures*, continued his meditation on China in transformation. Set in Datong, a grey provincial city caught amid mass demolition and construction, *Unknown Pleasures* traces the story of two delinquent teenagers who live on a diet of saccharine Chinese pop music, karaoke, *Pulp Fiction* and Coca-Cola while entertaining pipe dreams of joining the army and becoming small-time gangsters. Shot entirely with the new cinematic medium of digital video, *Unknown Pleasures* also marked a major step in the development of digital film-making in China.

In the 1990s, as unprecedented waves of migrant workers flocked China's urban centres from the countryside, Xiao Shan and countless others like him abandoned their hometowns to pursue new dreams in Beijing, Shanghai, Shenzhen and elsewhere. But what was the fate of all those small towns left behind for the big cities? Jia Zhangke's 'Hometown Trilogy' is an attempt to reexamine the transformation and fate of those places and people – and his own attempt to finally return home. At the heart of this book lies an exploration into the historical contexts of his films, the literary and cinematic intertexts with which they form dialogue, the thematic and philosophical hubs around which his filmic universe revolves, and the visual language that makes Jia's work so strikingly unique.

Each chapter is composed of close readings of crucial moments in each of the three films, through which I highlight Jia's use of editing, cinematic language and *mise en scène*, while, at the same time, teasing out the central narrative themes of destruction and change, stagnation and movement, political culture versus popular culture, and, of course, the ceaseless search for home.

2 Xiao Wu

In 1996 Jia Zhangke, then still a student at the Beijing Film Academy, brought *Xiao Shan Going Home* to Hong Kong to participate in the 2nd Annual Hong Kong Independent Short Film and Video Film Festival. The film not only took the Gold Prize at the festival, but the trip would ultimately prove to have a decisive impact on the future trajectory of Jia's career as a film-maker. This is not only because of the recognition and affirmation the film's success at the festival provided, but because it would also be where Jia would first meet a group of film-makers who would become core members of his collaborative team – including Chow Keung, Li Kit-Ming and Nelson Yu Lik Wai. All three were Hong Kong natives who had studied abroad (Chow in New York, Li in Paris and Yu in Belgium) and amassed rich experience in the Hong Kong film industry. When they saw *Xiao Shan Going Home* and met Jia Zhangke an immediate bond was formed. This was especially true of Nelson Yu Lik Wai, whose own short documentary film *Neon Goddesses* (*Meili de hunpo*) (1996) was also being screened at the same festival. Jia and Yu felt a strong camaraderie based on their mutual respect for each other's work and shared admiration for the films of Robert Bresson.[14] In Yu's *Neon Goddesses*, a documentary about three women in Beijing, several themes including a strong attention to popular music (the first five minutes of the film eschew dialogue completely in favour of a virtual arsenal of pop music references) and depictions of local 'clamp downs' on vice would all become signature elements of Jia's later films.[15]

Later in 1996, Jia and Yu joined with Li Kit-Ming's newly formed Hu Tong Communications, a Hong Kong-based company focused on independent film production – their first collaboration was what would be Jia Zhangke's feature-length debut film, *Xiao*

Wu. While Jia certainly had passion, drive and vision, his rapid rise and success surely has much to do with the experience, professionalism and international training of his core Hong Kong production team; together they created a dynamic not unlike that seen during the early years of the New Taiwan Cinema movement when locally trained directors (like Hou Hsiao-hsien) began to collaborate with a group of film-makers trained abroad (such as Edward Yang). With a partnership formed just on the eve of the historic 1997 handover of Hong Kong, the relationship between Jia and his Hong Kong partners would foreshadow the rapid integration of the Hong Kong and PRC film industries in the post-handover years. At the same time, this particular trans-China cinematic collaboration would go on to produce some of the most exciting and visionary cinematic works of contemporary Chinese cinema.

The story behind *Xiao Wu*, much like that of the main protagonist, also had humble beginnings. With a strategy of 'starting out small', the film-makers planned on beginning their collaboration with a low-budget short film. Jia wrote a screenplay, borrowing the title from F. Scott Fitzgerald's classic novel *Tender is the Night* (1934), that depicted a young couple's first night together in a hotel room. The short was intended to run thirty minutes, feature only two actors and use exclusively interior shots, depicting events transpiring over the course of a single night. Production was set to begin just after the Chinese New Year, but when Jia Zhangke brought Yu Lik Wai to his hometown of Fenyang for the holiday everything changed. It had been a year and a half since the aspiring director had been home and, struck by the monumental changes taking place there – from the widespread demolition of old buildings to the more subtle personal changes affecting his old friends – Jia was immediately driven to capture what was happening to his hometown.

Jia abandoned the original project for a new screenplay, which was to focus on a handicraftsman – perhaps a tailor or a metalworker – and explore the various pressures he would face amid the widespread changes going on. Eventually, Jia would settle on a pickpocket as his protagonist. Although I will argue later that *fictional* models from literature and cinema proved extremely influential in the creation of Xiao Wu, Jia did describe an old friend of his that served as inspiration for the lead character:

There was a rather rough model for Xiao Wu; he was an old buddy of mine, a 'sworn brother' who we called 'Donkey'. Another one of our buddies in the group was a police officer and he always kept an eye on Donkey. One day he told me that Donkey was really unbelievable – always carrying on about philosophy. What he meant by philosophy were things like; why do people live and other big metaphysical questions. I thought it was funny and gradually realised that even pickpockets have their system of honour. He may have had all kinds of moral baggage, but he still ponders his fate, which is where his honour lies.[16]

In the end, the film would trace several days in the life of a pickpocket during the time before and after the wedding of his one-time best friend. As the wedding draws near and eventually recedes into the distance, the protagonist Xiao Wu must negotiate his way through a maze of shifting relationships. This attraction to characters facing a sea of social, economic, cultural and environmental changes would go on to play an important role in Jia's trilogy, as well as his later films. During a 2006 forum held at Fenyang Middle School, leading PRC cultural critic Wang Hui spoke of the role of change and transformation in Jia's films:

the central motif of all of Jia Zhangke's films is change. This is true not only for *Still Life*, but from *Xiao Wu* all the way up to *The World*, the theme of change has inundated all of the living environments and relationships. All of the various narrative elements revolve around and are set in motion by change; the native home is in the process of disappearing, marriages, neighborhoods, relationships with friends and family are all in a state of change. And thus, attached to this theme of change and uncertainty is a search for stability and conviction. But in the end, what one finds is also in a state of flux, 'discovery' itself becomes a form of self-denial, or one could say that 'searching' is only but another form of self-denial.[17]

Shot in just twenty-one days, *Xiao Wu* would be completed in 1997, the same year Jia Zhangke graduated from the prestigious Beijing Film Academy. In fact, the film's opening credits bear the production title 'Beijing Film Academy Student Film', a reminder of just how impressive Jia's feat truly was. The film announced the arrival of Jia Zhangke as a important rising cinematic talent and garnered honours at film festivals around the world, including Berlin (Wolfgang Staudte and Netpac Awards), Brussels (Prix de l'Age d'Or), Pusan (New Current Prize), Vancouver (Dragon & Tiger Prize), Nantes (Best Film), San Francisco (Skyy Prize) and Rimini (Grand Prize). *Xiao Wu* was banned in China, but the handful of private screenings and bootleg editions that circulated were enough to build up an intense interest in the film among cinephiles, students and academics. 'Among all the banned films in China,' declared actor, director and critic Zhang Xianmin, '*Xiao Wu* is the most famous of them all; discussions of the film have inundated the internet and the screenplay was even published in a magazine.'[18] The DVD edition of *Xiao Wu* was belatedly released in China during 2005, a telling signpost of the changing terrain of the film industry in China, where Jia was increasingly being recognised as one of the most important post-Fifth Generation directors.

Part of the reason Jia's film was so revolutionary had to do with his own breed of cinematic realism that rejected earlier models of both the socialist-realist tradition and the work of Fifth Generation film-makers. Jia wanted to provide a glimpse of the true reality playing out in China's county towns, a reality often eschewed in favour of glamorous portraits of the urban metropolis or idyllic images of an idealised countryside. He set out to accomplish this with a stripped-down film aesthetic that drew heavily from documentary film traditions. In an interview with Zhang Yaxuan, cinematographer Nelson Yu Lik Wai spoke in detail about *Xiao Wu*'s documentary-esque shooting style:

[*Xiao Wu*] utilised all those things I learned about documentary film-making, such as clandestine shooting, shooting on the run and other methods arranged by the producers – but we certainly drew quite heavily from documentary shooting methods. Because there are very few films produced [in Shanxi], the locals always got excited and quite curious at the sight of the movie camera, they would tend to huddle together off to one side watching. We thought of all kinds of techniques to avoid this, even considering getting another group of people to create a scene nearby to draw their attention away, but nothing really worked.

   So we had no choice but to wait . . . we would just kill time until the crowds all tired out and went home to eat. We had to do our best to avoid environments that were overly complicated. And in cases where that was impossible, we had to find other methods, like hiding the camera or appropriating guerrilla film-making techniques – shooting quickly and then hightailing it out of there – all of these are quite similar to documentary film styles.[19]

In the end, the edgy hand-held camera work that punctuates *Xiao Wu*'s visual style does not distract as much as complement the overarching vision of the film, with the unpolished images reinforcing the gritty nature of the story and the dark reality the protagonist finds himself enmeshed in. According to Jia, more than two-thirds of the film uses hand-held shot.[20] At times, the swaying camera movements also seem to work in concert with Xiao Wu's distinctive swagger as he unassumingly prowls the streets of Fenyang. The use of documentary film techniques also helped establish Jia's somewhat hybrid form, which would stylistically borrow from both narrative and documentary traditions. (This hybrid style would be pushed even further with several of Jia's later films, such as *Useless* (*Wuyong*) [2007] and *24 City* (*Ershisi chengji*) [2008], which would more consciously challenge traditional divisions between narrative and documentary film categories.) The pacing of various shot and scene lengths and overall rhythm of the film also works to accentuate the story. As Chris Berry has noted, 'When Xiao Wu is attempting to take the initiative or assert himself, the pace is relatively fast and dynamic. But when he runs into obstacles, it slows.'[21] All of this points to the painstaking manner in which Jia, cinematographer Yu Lik Wai and their collaborators manipulate framing, pacing, composition and editing not simply in service of style but in order to complement the characters and their predicaments.

The sound design of *Xiao Wu* emphasises this same realist aesthetic. Whereas most mainstream films strive for clarity and clear dialogue in sound recording, Jia repeated requested his soundperson add more clamour to the film's soundscape, highlighting sounds from bicycles and passing traffic, television and radio broadcasts, background dialogue and various other forms of ambient noise. Such a strategy was in such conflict to what sound designers traditionally hope to accomplish that Jia even got into a well-documented row with the original sound recorder, Lin Xiaoling, who felt her professional reputation would be compromised if she followed the director's demands to repeatedly make the sound quality 'even coarser'. Eventually Lin left the shoot to be replaced by Zhang Yang, who would continue to work with Jia for most of his future projects.[22] As another facet of his drive for authenticity, Jia Zhangke also aimed to discard the proper Mandarin dialogue track endorsed by state-sponsored film studios in favour of local dialects that capture the genuine voice and speech cadence of real people. Regarding this conspicuous break with the long-entrenched language policies of the PRC, Kevin Lee wrote, 'It is as if Jia is personally compensating for seven decades of Chinese movies that have been dubbed in the standard Mandarin dialect in accordance with Government language policy.'[23] This approach, however, is not without its own problematics and contradictions. One of the most striking examples comes via Jia's casting choice of Wang Hongwei in the lead role. A native of the city Anyang in Henan province (the off-screen hometown of *Xiao Shan Going Home*), Wang never speaks the local Shanxi dialect in *Xiao Wu* – all of his lines are spoken in his own Anyang dialect while most of the other characters speak Shanxi dialect.[24] Aside from those from Shanxi or Henan, most audiences (especially international audiences) never notice the lead characters are speaking different dialects to one another, but we should not forget that Jia's ambitious challenge to the artificial hegemony of the Chinese language as represented by standard Mandarin is, in fact, another construction. The use of non-authentic dialects to produce the illusion of authenticity is but one example of how *Xiao Wu* creates a documentary-esque mood through meticulous employment of various aspects of the cinematic apparatus.[25]

Xiao Wu begins with one of the most brilliant opening sequences in contemporary cinema. With sparse dialogue, Jia uses a series of shots that quickly bring us into the protagonist's world, boldly sketching out his character and profession. In the first shot we can see a factory smokestack in the distance surrounded by fields, which, as Xiaoping Lin argues, 'link[s] the youthful protagonist with China's socialist past'[26] and serves as a distant reminder of the industrial-agricultural past from which Xiao Wu (and China) is emerging. In the foreground is in an extreme close-up of Xiao Wu's hand striking a match as he waits for a bus. As Jia has commented, 'I decided to open the film with a shot of his hands because he is a pickpocket, a thief, and his hands are the tools of his trade.'[27] In the following shot, we see Xiao Wu's hands from a reverse angle, as he lights up his cigarette.

The package of matches in his hand actually has 'Shanxi' written on it. I decided to add this prop in order to provide a spatial reference point to the viewers, which is very important. The whole issue of locale was extremely close to me when I made this film, and I wanted to highlight the fact that this was a story about Shanxi. It was really a rarity for a camera crew to come to a place like Shanxi and face the reality there, so I wanted to make this clear from the beginning. So the hands for the thief and the matches for Shanxi.[28]

The protagonist extends his arms, displaying the conspicuously oversized jacket sleeves, which have been cuffed over, and in the background is the highway, the road linking the rural with the urban, and the path to Xiao Wu's future.

Xiao Wu quickly hops on to a small private mini-bus heading for downtown Fenyang. As he climbs aboard, we are offered another close-up of Xiao Wu's arm, this time exposing a tattoo with the characters *younan tongdang*, or 'in times of difficulty share the burden', a further exposition of the character's shady roots. As the protagonist comes into full view it also becomes apparent that this is not the tall handsome leading man we are accustomed to encountering in the cinema. Xiao Wu's features and dress transmit not charisma but the kind of unassuming average-ness perfect for a pickpocket that needs to disappear into a crowd. At the same time, Xiao Wu's aura of mild homeliness, damaged self-esteem and repressed emotion also serves as a direct challenge to Hollywood-style leading man formulas. Once aboard he refuses to buy a ticket, claiming to be a policeman, and finds a seat beside a middle-aged man in a Mao jacket. Within seconds Xiao Wu's probing left hand extends from beneath his folded arms, finding its way into the man's pocket to lift his wallet. The theft, the first of the film (or second, if you count the bus ticket), is carried out under the gaze of the great leader, Chairman Mao Zedong, who appears laminated and hanging

Striking up before the industrial past and lighting up before the road to the future

from the bus's rear-view mirror – a nostalgic amulet of the past ironically watching over the ruins of a failed socialist utopia.

This opening sequence can be seen as a prelude to the film proper, which is devoted to the protagonist's relationships in Fenyang. But it is in this compact sequence that Jia Zhangke already begins to visually sketch out the key traits of his protagonist's personality. We should also not overlook the use of seemingly random street scenes in this sequence, such as the opening shot of a rural family waiting by the roadside seeing off their daughter. The image, one of the numerous shots of bystanders captured during the shoot, deeply moved the director with the way in which it conveyed the 'sadness of leaving'.[29] The shot also serves as another example of the film's hybrid identity, weaving essentially documentary film footage into the fabric of a narrative story. The departure, however, is not just that of the daughter, but also a farewell to the countryside, an era and a way of life. The unified nuclear family emerging from China's agricultural past also stands in direct opposition to the image of Xiao Wu's own shattered family, which will bring the film to its tragic conclusion.

Friends, lovers and family

Xiao Wu is structured around the protagonist's relationships with different groups of people in his life. The three sections focus on Xiao

Medium close-up of Xiao Wu's left hand lifting a wallet as Chairman Mao looks on

Wu's relationships with his former best friend, his lover and his family, with each cinematic chapter tracing the rapid shift and dissolution of those relationships. In the first section, we are presented with Jin Xiaoyong, Xiao Wu's childhood friend and a former pickpocket that used to run the streets with the protagonist. Xiaoyong has long since given up his old calling for larger enterprises, such as trading cigarettes and running a nightclub, which have made him into something of a local celebrity. With his newfound social status among the nouveau riche, Xiaoyong has distanced himself from his shady past . . . and his old friend Xiao Wu. It is Xiao Wu's discovery that he has not been invited to Xiaoyong's wedding that triggers the film's first conflict and interpersonal breakdown, setting in motion a destructive domino effect that carries through for the rest of the film.

Jia Zhangke is meticulous in setting up a series of visual cues that link the two estranged friends. In one early scene Xiaoyong stops before a brick wall in his family's courtyard and gently pats the surface. Several scenes later we see Xiao Wu repeating an almost identical action. Barely noticeable during a casual viewing, the brick wall actually bears the scrawled names of Xiao Wu and Xiaoyong, along with dates and height markings. These scenes set up a strong parallelism between the two characters as they revisit their common past and Jia takes us on a tour of a key site in his cinematic hometown. This type of visual syncretism is further enhanced in later scenes when Xiao Wu discovers that he has (unconsciously?) lifted his friend's musical cigarette lighter at the exact moment Xiaoyong discovers it is missing.

Jia links the characters through not only a meticulously structured series of similar actions, but also by highlighting their differences in similar situations. Early in the film we see Xiaoyong delivering a long statement on camera to the local Fenyang Television station (FYTV). While Xiaoyong's slightly awkward appearance, speaking in a thick Shanxi dialect, can hardly qualify as on-screen charisma, it stands in stark opposition to a similar scene where Santu,

Jin Xiaoyong caressing the wall that represents his childhood and past

Close-up of wall

Xiao Wu repeating the same motion

a young member of Xiao Wu's gang, is targeted by a roving reporter to make a comment about the government 'clamp down' on crime. In contrast to Xiaoyong, who courts the media with cigarettes and favours, Xiao Wu aggressively grabs Santu and pulls him away from the cameras and microphones. Whereas Xiaoyong has learned to harness the media's powers of legitimisation for his own purposes, Xiao Wu has failed to make the adaptation to this new world, choosing instead to remain in the shadows.

This juxtaposition is revisited again after the old friends' meeting on the eve of Xiaoyong's wedding. They part ways in disharmony as Xiao Wu pulls up his old buddy's sleeve and barks at him, 'Take a look at your arm!' Although Jia does not give us a close-up of Xiaoyong's arm (a further denial of their present connection), on his forearm is a tattoo of a small dragon accompanied by the Chinese characters *youfu tongxiang*, 'in times of happiness share the good fortune'. This is the second half of the couplet displayed earlier on Xiao Wu's arm – the promise of brotherhood once etched in blood is here negated as Xiaoyong harvests his own good fortune, exiling Xiao Wu (and the symbolic bearer of ill fortune) from his life. In the following scene, Xiao Wu is alone in a local restaurant drinking away his sorrows; he lights a cigarette with the stolen lighter just as Xiaoyong is searching for the same missing lighter. Both characters are watching the local FYTV station broadcast of a special segment

Jin Xiaoyong courting the media as Xiao Wu runs away from it about Jin Xiaoyong's wedding, that very segment seen being recorded earlier that day. Understated, realistic and naturally unfolding, the sequence highlights the film's ability to sketch out the interconnections between these two characters – and the rift between them – through a series of subtle yet powerful juxtapositions of setting, movement and framing. The seemingly ubiquitous presence of FYTV (not to mention radio and other forms of mass media that repeatedly bleed into the soundtrack) and its legitimising power speaks to the ways in which local media culture has infiltrated the people's lives – even in a small town like Fenyang. Thanks to this shift, even the most quotidian of events – from Xiaoyong's wedding announcement to Xiao Wu's fleeting appearance on FYTV during a report on 'clamping down' – become reproduced and amplified, as do the pride and shame associated with such events.

At the end of the first section of the film, Jia Zhangke gives us sudden blackout that he holds for several seconds as a warped electronic version of Beethoven's 'Für Elise' emits from the stolen lighter, until it eventually peters out and dies. As the music trails off we are also hit with the symbolic demise of the friendship Xiao Wu once held so dear. But as the film progresses, Jia sets up linkages

Jin Xiaoyong on FYTV

between one failed relationship and the next, highlighting the role of a series of gifts that serve as destructive bridges between each section.

Immediately, we are taken into the second part of the film, which deals with Xiao Wu's relationship with Hu Meimei, a bar girl working at a karaoke club called Little Shanghai. Xiao Wu's awkwardness and inability to find his place in the new social order is highlighted through his unwillingness to sing or dance. Xiao Wu also does not know where to take Meimei when the Madame lets him take her out of the club. Clearly uncomfortable and unaccustomed to the practices of this seedy world, it quickly becomes evident that Xiao Wu's patronage of the karaoke bar is a direct attempt to battle the loneliness and loss felt by Xiaoyong's rejection. In the sequences that follow, we witness their 'courtship', which gains momentum after Xiao Wu visits Meimei at her dormitory when she falls ill. Xiao Wu brings Meimei a hot water bottle and the couple exchange songs, Meimei sings a solo version of Faye Wang's 'Sky' ('Tiankong') while Xiao Wu has no recourse but open his stolen lighter and let it play its digital rendition of 'Für Elise'. Here the stolen token from Xiao Wu's failed friendship becomes a tool for building his new relationship; as the robotic strains of Beethoven's music sound, Meimei curls up to Xiao Wu in her bed and, for the very first time, they embrace. However, one cannot forget the message left over from the first chapter of the film. Though the replaying of 'Für Elise' seems to facilitate romance for Xiao Wu, its soulless, mechanical reproduction serves as a powerful indicator that this new relationship may not be one based on genuine feelings . . . and, besides, though Xiao Wu may have replaced its battery, we already know that the musical lighter is prone to failure.

It is during this second segment, exactly half way through the film, that Jia Zhangke presents us with one of the film's most moving sequences when Xiao Wu visits an empty bathhouse. His visit to the bathhouse seems to be directly inspired by Meimei's comment on his hygiene in an earlier scene. Yu's camera highlights the nude body of the protagonist as he slowly walks through the bathhouse, eventually

crawling to a large tub. Using a series of long takes to accentuate this important moment in the character's development, it is here that Xiao Wu, naked and alone for the first time in the film, begins to open up and sing.

This is a turning point for the character who, unencumbered by his oversized suit, the large, thick-rimmed glasses that he hides behind and the labyrinth of social relationships in which he is lost, finally exposes another side of himself through the lyrics of 'Raining Heart' ('Xin yu'). What is interesting is that this is the very song that was dedicated to Jin Xiaoyong on FYTV just before his wedding. It is also the same song that Meimei asked Xiao Wu to sing during his first visit to the karaoke bar, which he declined. In a gesture that seems to simultaneously celebrate Xiaoyong's wedding while mourning the loss of their friendship, Xiao Wu's echoing voice fills the open bathhouse. The song also represents a belated offering to Meimei – the firsts step in his active pursuit of her – Xiao Wu finally begins to take down the walls he has built up around himself. The extended take that ends the sequence highlights the scene's overall importance in the narrative arc of the film. Jia then presents us with a rapid montage sequence of Xiao Wu singing, dancing, drinking, having dinner with his friends – all culminating in the purchase of a ring. This is the first time in the film that Xiao Wu begins to smile and come out of his shell, fully opening himself up to

Xiao Wu and Hu Meimei in the karaoke room at Little Shanghai and Xiao Wu singing 'Raining Heart' at the public bathhouse the surrounding social group, and even purchasing a beeper at Meimei's suggestion so she can always get in touch with him.

But the optimism expressed in the film's central bathhouse scene is all but shattered with Meimei's abandonment of Xiao Wu (apparently to run off with a wealthy Shanxi businessman), leaving the protagonist even more desperate and alone. The reason for their failed relationship lies in part simply with the practical forces that brought them together – Xiao Wu earns (steals) money to impress Meimei, while Meimei sells herself to earn money. As Cui Shuqin has noted, Xiao Wu 'and the singing girl sense themselves falling in love, but they fail to realize that their relationship is grounded on a commercial transaction'.[30] With Meimei's departure, the film moves into its third act, which deals with Xiao Wu's relationship with his family. The shortest and most brutal segment of the film, the final chapter follows Xiao Wu as he returns home only to get in a fight with his parents, that ultimately leads to his being driven out of his home by his father wielding a club.

While each segment is seemingly self-contained in that primary characters of earlier segments rarely reappear in latter sections, Jia carefully ties each interpersonal breakdown to the previous one.[31] He accomplishes this by way of a series of material exchanges in each section, the consequences of which reverberate in latter sequences of the film. The wedding gift given to Xiaoyong in part one is only

'No need to ever come back to this house!' Xiao Wu driven away by his father and dangling

returned to Xiao Wu in part two. It is delivered by one of Xiaoyong's cronies (played by none other than Jia Zhangke in a cameo) to Xiao Wu at Little Shanghai, in the presence of Meimei with a comment that 'Xiaoyong said your money isn't clean.' Occurring just a few scenes before Meimei's disappearance, this scene not only represents Xiaoyong's final blow to Xiao Wu, but also signals the beginning of Meimei's disillusionment with her lover. Thus the forces that both bring Xiao Wu and Meimei together and tear them apart are intricately tied to a pair of items linked to Xiaoyong – the musical lighter and the cash wedding gift.

Likewise, there are two props from Xiao Wu's relationship with Meimei that drive the devastating final scenes of the film. First, there is the wedding ring originally intended for Meimei that Xiao Wu decides to give to his mother. It is his discovery that she has given it away to his sister-in-law that fuels the final argument between Xiao Wu and his parents, ending in his ejection from the family. And then there is the beeper that Meimei asked Xiao Wu to buy so she could always get in touch with him. Not only does the beeper fail to bring him closer to his lover, but when it suddenly goes off with a weather update as Xiao Wu is lifting a wallet, it becomes the direct impetus to his arrest. The connection between material exchange and Xiao Wu's downfall can easily be read as a critique of capitalism and the rapid drive towards materialism gripping China in the late 1990s. The irony is that not only does no one want Xiao Wu's gifts and commodities – Xiaoyong doesn't want his money, Meimei and his mother do not want his ring – but it is precisely these commodities that play a key role in further alienating the hero and leading to the destruction of his relationships with those around him.

Another, often neglected, example of material exchange in the film comes in the form of the stolen identification cards that Xiao Wu lifts from his victims. Having no use for the ID cards and apparently aware of how difficult it is to replace them, Xiao Wu drops these cards – a record of his crimes – into street-side post boxes, where they eventually make their way into the hands of Hao Yongliang

(Liang Yonghao), a senior policeman who has already had previous run-ins with Xiao Wu and his gang – Xiao Wu even refers to Hao as 'teacher' when they run into one another. In several separate scenes we see Hao at his desk in the police station in the evening, solemnly going through a pile of missing ID cards. Each sequence is directly tied to another one of Xiao Wu's crime sprees, one to get together enough cash for Xiaoyong's wedding present, another to buy Meimei her ring. What is interesting is that, of his spoils, the single items that Xiao Wu consistently dispenses with are these ID and residence cards – signatures of one's identity and place in the world, precisely what Xiao Wu seems to lack as he blindly drifts.

Xiao Wu's own value system is punctuated by the sequence of each relationship, screen time devoted to each and degree of emotional devastation felt by Xiao Wu after each relationship falls apart. Inverting traditional Confucian values where filial piety comes first, the place of the family seems to come last in the protagonist's world. Xiao Wu's relationship with his parents and siblings is replaced by a romanticised conception of 'brotherhood' inspired by gangster movies and martial arts novels.[32] It is also telling that within this network of blistered connections and failed relationships, Xiao Wu himself comes last. It is no accident that the original intended title of the film, 'Jin Xiaoyong's Buddy, Hu Meimei's Sugardaddy, and Liang Changyou's Son: Xiao Wu', maps the protagonist's identity only vis-à-vis his relationship with those around him.[33] This early title also divulges the narrative structure of the film, making explicit just how central these relationships are to Jia's vision of the film. The construction of Xiao Wu's identity is contingent upon those around him and when those relationships fall apart, he is left with nothing.

Intertextual interventions

Intricately tied to the structure and vision of *Xiao Wu* are the intertextual ties between Jia's film and the work of some of his cinematic heroes, especially Robert Bresson's *Pickpocket* (1959) and

Vittorio De Sica's *Bicycle Thieves* (1948). Jia reflected on this
connection during an interview with Lin Xudong:

Later, when I thought back, I realised that my interest in this type of
character was probably related to an unconscious factor: two of the directors
that proved to have the greatest impact on my work, Vittorio De Sica and
Robert Bresson both made films depicting thieves – *Bicycle Thieves* and
Pickpocket. Those were two of my favourite films back when I was still in
school. But I only really became conscious of this influence [on *Xiao Wu*] later;
I wasn't at all aware of it when I was writing the screenplay.[34]

In the end, however, it is much more than the common theme of the
thief/pickpocket that cements Jia's indebtedness to Bresson and De
Sica. *Xiao Wu* also shares a similar neo-realist aesthetic, employment
of exclusively non-professional actors, as well as a similar social
backdrop of poverty and desperation during a period of major
historical transition. For De Sica this backdrop was Italy's period of
postwar rebuilding, while for Jia this is China's post-socialist
transitional period. In both cases, there is also a common interest in
using genuine locations, with special attention to the dilapidated
architecture and semi-demolished buildings against which the
protagonists try to find their way. Like the neo-realists, locations are
so central to Jia's cinematic universe – such as the Little Shanghai
karaoke parlour where Xiao Wu first meets Meimei, the street-side
noodle stall where Xiao Wu congregates with his young gang, or
Geng Sheng's shop which teeters on the verge of demolition.
These sites become essential components of the film's *mise en scène*,
taking on an importance almost as significant as the characters
themselves. Further attesting to the neo-realist connection is the fact
that in some international markets, *Xiao Wu* even appeared with the
alternate title *Pickpocket* or *Artisan Pickpocket* in a tribute to
Bresson's masterpiece.

The true urtext for *Xiao Wu*, however, lies in one of the classic
works of modern Chinese literature, Lu Xun's *The True Story of Ah*

Q (*Ah Q zheng zhuan*) (1921). A satiric literary critique of the Chinese national character, Lu Xun's story has become a key text in modern China. Because of his power as a cultural symbol and the deep resonances he has inspired over the past three-quarters of a century, Ah Q has inspired countless adaptations, rewrites and imitations, from 1950's *Miss Modern: The Biography of Miss Ah Q* (*Modeng xiaojie: Ah Q xiaojie zhuan*) to 1994's *Sequel to the True Story of Ah Q* (*Ah Q houzhuan*).[35] One of the most fascinating reinventions comes with *Xiao Wu*, which I suggest is actually a post-socialist reimagination of China's ultimate allegorical anti-hero – Ah Q.

In *The True Story of Ah Q*, the identity of the main character is a chief point of contention. As the author writes,

The third difficulty I encountered in writing this work was that I don't know how Ah Q's personal name should be written either. During his lifetime everybody called him Ah Quei, but after his death not a soul mentioned Ah Quei again; for he was obviously not one of those whose name is 'preserved on bamboo tablets and silk.' If there is any question of preserving his name, this essay must be the first attempt at doing so.[36]

In fact, Lu Xun devoted the entire introductory section of his landmark story to a humorous, satiric and tragic rumination on the origins and possible meanings of Ah Q's name. It is, in fact, not much of a name but a placeholder. In Xiao Wu, the protagonist's name may not be a point of contention, but both characters share in their common lack of identity and the way in which their relationships determine their respective place – or lack of place – in the world. As shown earlier, Xiao Wu's identity is established only in relation to those around him and it is a similar network of failed relationships that also drives Lu Xun's *The True Story of Ah Q*. Among such examples stands the famous scene at the beginning of the story where Ah Q is driven out of the Zhao household and forced to renounce any claim to the Zhao surname. Or Ah Q's infamous attempt to make an advance on Aunt Wu that results in an embarrassing rejection for the protagonist. Both episodes seem to manifest themselves in Jia Zhangke's film.

Among Ah Q's traits, one of the most discussed is his *jingshen shengli fa*, or 'spiritual victory complex', which has gone on to be frequently referenced as an embodiment of the negative traits of the Chinese national character. The 'spiritual victory complex' as conceived by Lu Xun refers to his protagonists' penchant for transforming failures into mental victories, often by way of projecting injustices suffered onto others in lower social positions. Such instances occur throughout Lu Xun's story and Jia Zhangke appropriates his own version of this complex for his character Xiao Wu.

Xiao Wu exemplifies this 'spiritual victory complex' in a fashion reminiscent of Ah Q: in the beginning of the film the wise smirk Xiao Wu displays as he gets away with impersonating a plainclothes police officer to avoid paying bus fare (top image); he berates a construction worker and turns off his electric saw while Meimei is trying to make a telephone call (centre image); or he gives his 'apprentice' Santu a hard time for being seen with a girl when Xiao Wu himself is still struggling for Meimei's affections (lower image). These typical Ah Qisms occur throughout the film and work to create a character that, not unlike Lu Xun's protagonist, appears weak and stubborn while eliciting a deep sympathy. Then there is, of course, Xiao Wu's chosen profession as a thief, a trade also taken up by Ah Q, which causes both of them to fall out of favour with their townspeople. And even similar secondary characters, such as *Xiao Wu*'s Santu, a member of Xiao Wu's gang of adolescent thieves, an earlier model of whom can be found in Xiao D in *The True Story of Ah Q*. Xiao D is portrayed by Lu Xun as yet another incarnation of the Ah Q spirit and Santu serves the same role in *Xiao Wu*. After putting up with Xiao Wu's criticisms, the moment his old buddy is imprisoned, Santu shows up interviewed on FYTV berating Xiao Wu as a 'scourge to society that should be locked up!' Santu's

Three images of Xiao Wu's
'spiritual victory complex'

comments not only further crush the already broken Xiao Wu, but his identical employment of the same 'spiritual victory complex' also cements his identity as Xiao Wu's double. At the same time, the sequence further displays both characters as reinventions of their true models, Ah Q and Xiao D.[37]

Although the influence of Lu Xun and his *True Story of Ah Q* is quite pervasive in modern Chinese culture, the stunning intertextual similarities point to *Xiao Wu* as a contemporary reinvention akin to what Gerard Genette has characterised as a form of *hypertextuality*, for the way in which the text elaborates or transforms an earlier work. While *Xiao Wu* shares numerous traits in common with its predecessor, from the series of failed relationships (the Zhao family/Jin Xiaoyong, Aunt Wu/Hu Meimei, Xiao D/Santu) to the shared characteristics ('spiritual victory complex' and 'rootlessness') and occupations (thieves) of the respective protagonists, one of the great testaments to Jia Zhangke's skill as an artist lies in his ability to carry out this *hypertextual* intervention using a cinematic form that feels completely rooted in the neo-realist tradition pioneered by De Sica and Bresson. As powerful a cultural symbol as Ah Q has been, he has almost always remained an allegorical caricature. *Xiao Wu*, however, elevates Ah Q to the realm of the real and does so in a manner that remains virtually transparent to most casual audiences.

Similarities aside, perhaps it is even more instructive to pinpoint how Xiao Wu stands unique from the prototype of Ah Q. For while the shadow of Lu Xun's anti-hero looms large, Xiao Wu stands as a far more self-conscious character, keenly aware of his surroundings and predicament. With this awareness comes a bleak defeatist outlook that stands in sharp contrast to Ah Q's 'ignorance-is-bliss' mentality; the ever-cheerful Ah Q is seemingly never aware of the gravity of the situations he finds himself in, not when he is denounced by his 'family', rejected by Aunt Wu, or even facing imminent execution. And unlike Ah Q, who is always submissive to power, Xiao Wu is markedly more subversive, consistently challenging engrained power structures while struggling to adhere to his own romanticised moral core (as evidenced by his notions of 'brotherhood' and taking the time to return stolen identification cards). Ah Q may be the model, but the character of Xiao Wu proves to be a more nuanced construction, imbued with a strong self-awareness, brooding pessimism, a flawed moral compass and the faint dreams of an idealist pushed to the very margins of society. As the film moves towards its conclusion and Xiao Wu's story inches towards its inevitable end, the implications of these characteristics ensure that this contemporary retelling of Ah Q will prove to be all the more tragic and devastating for the protagonist.

Revolution reconsidered

During the climactic final scene in *Xiao Wu*, the protagonist is finally arrested. Bound and led down the main street of his hometown of Fenyang, Xiao Wu is temporarily handcuffed to a telephone pole while Officer Hao, who is in charge of him, goes off to run an errand. Shackled and squatting like a dog, Xiao Wu is gradually surrounded by a group of onlookers who have come to gawk at the spectacle. This is the final tragedy in the life of Xiao Wu. Over the course of the film, we witness the destruction of Xiao Wu's relationships with his friends, girlfriend and family – his arrest is the final blow. As Xiao Wu spirals downward we are also privy to the physical destruction of his hometown as the shops and homes along the main street are prepared for demolition. This dismantling of Xiao Wu's environment on the eve of his personal downfall speaks powerfully to the innate parallelism Jia establishes between his characters and their environments. Xiao Wu's moral system is just as useless and outdated as the buildings now marked for destruction. Handcuffed in a public display that announces his guilt to his fellow townspeople, the gesture seems to almost echo the signs of *chai* (demolish) scrawled on the buildings marked to be torn down.

The shackling is carried out by Hao Yongliang, the older policeman who is the recipient of the stolen identification cards Xiao Wu dropped in the mailbox. As a symbol of state power, the benevolence, sensitivity and kindness that the policeman displays throughout the film comes as a surprise in a film otherwise laden with subversive content and themes, including portrayals of pickpockets, prostitutes and corruption. At the same time, we should not forget the way in which the policeman encourages Xiao Wu to emulate his old buddy Xiaoyong – an even bigger thief – a detail that displays the ways in which state power sides with economic power. We should also not forget that it is he who commits this final, almost casual, act of humiliation against Xiao Wu. For Xiao Wu, who throughout the film thrives on his guise of 'average-ness' and ability to disappear in a crowd of anonymity, it is this public exhibition that represents the ultimate pain and disgrace. When director Martin Scorsese described the film, he also made special mention of that final tragic scene where the policeman handcuffs Xiao Wu to a pole: 'There's nothing sentimental about Wang Hongwei's performance or about Jia's approach to him, and somehow that makes the end of the film, where the protagonist is arrested, chained, and exposed to public ridicule, all the more devastating.'[38]

A microcosm of this ending actually occurs at the beginning of the film, when Xiao Wu first arrives back in Fenyang and sees a crowd of onlookers gawking at a newly posted announcement declaring the city government's new policy on 'clamping down' on crime.[39] During an interview I did with Jia Zhangke in 2002, I asked him to talk about that final scene where Xiao Wu is chained to a telephone pole and forced to confront the eyes of a crowd of onlookers:

In the original script the ending was supposed to be of the old police officer leading Xiao Wu through the street, eventually disappearing into a crowd. But as I was shooting, I was never really completely satisfied with this original ending. It is a safe ending, but also a rather mediocre one. During the twenty days of the shoot I was constantly trying to come up with a better ending. Suddenly one day when we were shooting a crowd started to gather around to watch us filming and I was struck with a kind of inspiration. I decided to shoot a crowd scene of people staring at him. I felt that in some way, this crowd could serve as a kind of bridge with the audience. Like the audience, the crowd is also spectators, but there is a shift in perspective. As soon as I thought of it I felt a kind of excitement. Naturally, I also thought of Lu Xun's[40] conception of the 'crowd'.[41]

The 'crowd' of onlookers is a motif that occurs throughout Lu Xun's fictional universe, staring at the madman in 'Diary of a Madman' ('Kuangren riji'), eagerly awaiting the execution in 'Medicine' ('Yao'), cheering at the legendary decapitation slide in 'Preface to *Call to Arms*' ('Nahan zixu') or gawking at Ah Q in disappointment when he gets shot instead of decapitated in *The True Story of Ah Q*. Within the cinematic apparatus, the crowd becomes not simply the observers of this display of public humiliation and violence, but also the object of the gaze as the camera turns on them. The shot/reverse shot sequence of Xiao Wu and the crowd further emphasises Xiao Wu's identity in relation to society (the crowd), who are here cut off from him, framed in separate shots. It is society that creates and destroys Xiao Wu. In sharp contrast to Jia's original script, which had Xiao Wu

Bound in public and forced to face the onlookers in *Xiao Wu* and *The True Story of Ah Q*

disappearing into a sea of people as he was led down a crowded street by the police officer, the revised ended actually reinforces Xiao Wu's isolation and alienation.

The brutal conclusion to *Xiao Wu* on the one hand seals its hypertextual connection to the *The True Story of Ah Q*; at the same time, the context also points to a new twist on Lu Xun's tale. Lu Xun's original story was set during a time of tumultuous political and social change – the end of the last dynastic era, the rise of the Republic, a rush towards westernisation and a time of social and economic uncertainty – *The True Story of Ah Q* is very much a portrait of Ah Q's struggle to gain a foothold against a backdrop of political revolution where even his own identity seemed to be at stake. Seventy-six years later, Jia Zhangke's *Xiao Wu* is set during a new revolution, but rather than political, it is an economic revolution, and one that has proceeded to shake the spiritual, moral and even physical foundation of everyone in and around Fenyang. As Xiao Wu's relationships collapse around him, so does the moral code of 'brotherhood' he thought he shared with Jin Xiaoyong, so do the values he thought his family shared and so does any chance of love in an environment where everything is a commodity. And as he squats shackled in public, signalling the end of the road for Xiao Wu, so his city enters into the throes of destruction and demolition as it makes way for the architectural

The 'crowd' gazing at the bound prisoner in *Xiao Wu* and *The True Story of Ah Q* juggernauts that will come with this new economic revolution. In the end, this new system of 'socialism with Chinese characteristics' not only leaves Xiao Wu behind, but also consumes China's traditional social structures and moral systems; but, unlike Ah Q, here there is very little irony.[42]

3 Platform

Originally intended as Jia Zhangke's first feature-length production, the director actually began work on the screenplay for *Platform* as early as 1995. The film called for a large cinematic canvas to portray the incredible social, economic and cultural changes in China during the 1980s. Jia knew this could never be undertaken on the paltry 200,000 yuan budget available, which came from his Hong Kong investor, Hu Tong Communications, along with Radiant Advertising, a local Shanxi advertising company which would cover the remainder of the budget. Jia opted instead to start with a smaller-scale project, which eventually became *Xiao Wu*. (The final cost for *Xiao Wu*, including post-production was closer to 380,000 yuan.) It was only after the critical success of *Xiao Wu* that Jia Zhangke and his collaborators were able to get the funding to finally undertake *Platform*. This time around, Jia's funding sources diversified considerably; in addition to Hong Kong's Hu Tong Communications, T-Mark, a Japanese production company run by iconic film-maker Takeshi Kitano (aka 'Beat Takeshi') came in as a major partner. Part of Jia's reason for going with T-Mark had to do with producer Shozo Ichiyama's longstanding relationship with Taiwan director Hou Hsiao-hsien, one of Jia's cinematic heroes from whom he drew much creative inspiration. In addition to Hong Kong and Japanese funding, *Platform* was also the recipient of a 700,000 franc subsidy from the French Ministry of Foreign Affairs. In an attempt to avoid the fate of *Xiao Wu*, Jia Zhangke also entered into talks with the Beijing and Shanghai Film Studios to co-produce. In order to change his status at the Film Bureau and attain a film production licence, *Platform* would have to be produced in cooperation with one of the official state-run film studios. And while talks initially seemed promising, both Beijing and Shanghai proved unsuccessful in their efforts to change Jia's status

– this ultimately ensured that as far as commercial Chinese release went, *Platform* would never leave the station.

Just as its production team was made up of a group of disparate international investors, so too *Platform*'s theatrical audience would be composed of almost exclusively international audiences. (Although denied commercial release in China, *Platform*, like Jia's other films, would enjoy a healthy audience in China via the bootleg DVD market.)

Platform seemed to make good on the promise hinted at in *Xiao Wu* and would be considered by many critics to be the first masterpiece by the young director. The film went on to win more

Cover image from one of the many bootleg VCD versions of *Platform* in China. This version bears the Warner Bros. label on the side and back and features a trio of charismatic stars, none of whom actually appear in the film. The running time of this version is 139 minutes, as one of the crucial scenes was cut out so it could fit on two discs than half a dozen major prizes at international film festivals, including the Don Quixote Award and FIPRESCI Prize at Fribourg, the Golden Montgolfiere at Nantes and the Netpac Award at Venice, where it was also nominated for a Golden Lion (an award Jia would finally take home six years later with *Still Life*). *Platform* was featured on top ten lists throughout Europe and Asia during the year of its international commercial release. Upon release international critics lauded the film with praise; Jonathan Rosenbaum hailed the film 'as one of the most impressive Chinese films I've ever seen' and J. Hoberman described it as 'one of the richest films of the past decade'.[43]

Like *Xiao Wu*, the film is also set primarily in Jia Zhangke's hometown of Fenyang, with the city itself becoming an increasingly central component in the director's cinematic universe (although numerous scenes were actually shot in the neighbouring town of Pingyao). Many of Jia's collaborators from the previous production returned for *Platform*, most notably lead actor Wang Hongwei and the core Hong Kong production team of Li Kit-Ming, Chow Keung and cinematographer Nelson Yu Lik Wai. And while it was still Yu behind the camera, the visual strategy and overall *mise en scène* of *Platform* was quite different from *Xiao Wu*. This time out the visual composition was dominated primarily by long shots, long takes, extremely limited camera movements and virtually no close-ups or hand-held shots. It was with this renewed approach on *Platform* that Jia's indebtedness to the masterworks of Ozu and Hou truly became evident. Jia's comments emphasise the function of the long take in his work:

The use of the long take highlights the clear stance that young directors have taken – that is, to objectively reveal what lies before their eyes, to maintain a distanced observation, to respect the various things that occur in a given time and space, to freely allow events to unfold without interference, to not guide the gaze of the audience and allow them to maintain their autonomy of observation. This consciousness of equality, respect for the individual, longing for freedom and other themes all inundate the cinematic language.[44]

And while the long take was certainly present in *Xiao Wu* (such as the karaoke scenes or the long three-minute shot in the public bathhouse), with *Platform* this approach also helped accentuate the historical distance of the subject matter in contrast to the urgency and contemporaneousness of *Xiao Wu*. With *Platform* Jia was clearly attempting to push the technique further and, in the process, prod his audiences to move away from cinematic models that allow them to remain in a more passive role.

The film included scenes taking place during each season over several years of narrative time, which called for three separate shoots that spanned nearly a year. The shoot also required the entire production to move between numerous locations in order to capture the action taking place in the second half of the film, as the troupe travels to various locales throughout northern China. The production design, which needed to convey the passage of time through changing fashions, hairstyles, pop music, propaganda slogans and set design, was overseen by Qiu Sheng. And although Jia had a much greater budget to work with as compared with his previous feature, considering the epic scale of *Platform*, funding was still tight. For the cast Jia drew heavily from his own crew and circle of friends. The troupe leader Xu was played by avant-garde poet Xi Chuan, actors Song Yongping and Liang Jingdong both doubled as art design consultants, and everyone from assistant director Gu Zheng to consultant Lin Xudong took parts in the cast.

Spanning just over a decade, *Platform* is an ode to China in the 1980s and the radical transformation society went through in the wake of the Cultural Revolution. In 1976 Mao Zedong died and the Cultural Revolution – a ten-year political maelstrom that pushed the cult of Mao and his policies to absurd new heights – finally came to an end. After a brief transition period, Deng Xiaoping bumped Mao's chosen successor Hua Guofeng from power in 1980 and proceeded to institute a series of sweeping new policies that would transform China's infrastructure and encourage a free market economy. *Platform* explores this era through the members of a song and dance troupe as they ride the waves of social and cultural change. The chief protagonists are two couples who are both members of the troupe, Cui Mingliang (Wang Hongwei) and his love interest Yin Ruijuan (Zhao Tao), and Zhang Jun (Liang Jingdong) and his steady girlfriend Zhong Ping (Yang Tianyi). Although none of the actors in the main cast were professionally trained, all had strong connections with Beijing's film-making community. Wang Hongwei was a former classmate of the director from the Beijing Film Academy who had previously been featured in *Xiao Shan Going Home* and *Xiao Wu*; Zhao Tao was a dancer who would subsequently go on to become one of Jia's core actors; Liang Jingdong was an art designer who had previously worked on *Xiao Wu* (as well as several of Jia's later productions); and Yang Tianyi was the director of *Old Men* (*Lao ren*), a 1999 documentary that has already claimed a place as one of the cornerstone works in the new Chinese underground documentary movement.

The film traces the development of these two couples as Zhang and Zhong go from a seemingly harmonious relationship to a sudden break-up and Cui and Yin go from tense estrangement to a sudden union in the final scenes of the film. But more than the fate of these four characters, *Platform* is interested in the human effects of large-scale political, economic and cultural change. As the song and dance troupe transforms from a government-sponsored work unit to a private for-profit organisation, fashions change, society transforms and Jia presents a masterfully observed epic on the clash between idealism and reality. In describing his film, Jia has expressed the film's exploration of how the reform era has impacted everyday people:

The Cultural Revolution generation always talks about how they lived through such a painful calamity in Chinese history, but I feel that the shock and incredible impact the decade of reform and economic commodification in the 1980s had on individuals was also extremely profound. ... you can't say that simply because that generation's material life is richer, their lives are happier. What I really want to focus on is, over the course of this transformation, who is paying the price? What kinds of people are paying the price?[45]

Set between 1979 and 1991, from the early days after the Cultural Revolution to just after the 1989 Tiananmen Square crackdown, *Platform* can be seen as the prequel to *Xiao Wu*. And although there is no continuity of story between the films, *Xiao Wu* can very much be seen as an extension of the historical timeline and topographical mapping sketched out in *Platform*. Read as a prequel, *Platform* displays the roots and development of the social malaise gripping the world of Xiao Wu and his friends, but *Platform* also goes much further, presenting a moving tone poem on time, transformation and the trauma lurking at the crossroads of socialism and capitalism.

   Platform is epic not only in historical scope and the physical terrain the protagonists travail, but also in terms of the film length. It is Jia Zhangke's single longest film to date and the first cut clocked in at 210 minutes. Jia eventually cut twenty minutes off the running time, submitting a 190-minute version to the Venice International Film Festival. The version that most audiences have seen, however, is the 150-minute cut, which was the version used for international theatrical as well as DVD release, and is also the director's preferred cut.[46] The primary difference between the final cut and the various extended versions lies in the removal of numerous scenes (or portions of scenes) that further elucidate the motivations behind various characters' actions. The final cut therefore features an overall aesthetic and cinematic language that is significantly more subtle, understated and difficult. Certain plot details that are very clearly delineated in the longer versions, need to be extracted from subtle hints in existing dialogue, or, in many cases, simply inferred from context. The result is a significantly different viewing experience between the different cuts, with the original version following much more closely traditional conventions of film narrative. Jia Zhangke hinted at the understated narrative approach employed in the final cut during an interview with Cheng Qingsong and Huang Ou:

During the long writing process I continually revised the screenplay. The most significant changes made were that in the original screenplay all of the characters' backstories and drives were very clearly delineated. Take for instance the character Yin Ruijuan; what eventually happened to her, why did she become a tax agent, how did she get there? The early version made all of that very clear. But when it came to the actual shoot I one day suddenly realized I couldn't go on like that. It became clear that there was a problem with the narrative and I halted production, I felt I had to change it; it struck me that anyone would understand the life journey of a girl – or a boy for that matter – living in a provincial city like that. There was no need to explain all those details, they simply weren't important.[47]

Other examples of how Jia cut scenes to streamline the narrative flow of the film include the handling of Cui Mingliang's affair with Li Xiaojuan, a dancer who joins the troupe with her twin sister during the latter stages of the film. In the extended version, there are two scenes the depict their break-up – the first at a roadside food stall where they sit in awkward silence until Li announces she is leaving, and the second scene where Cui sees her off as she boards a bus to Shiling. Both scenes were removed from the final cut, effectively leaving the audience to deduce the cause and manner of their break-up. The removal of these transitional scenes effectively brings an economy and elegance to the narrative and overall structure of the film; at the same time setting up a temporal strategy that sometimes challenges film conventions.[48]

Other changes that occurred only after production began included the addition of the theme of departure and homecoming as a key structuring device to trace the journey of the protagonists as they leave Fenyang and return. It was also at the eleventh hour – actually *after* principal shooting had begun – that Jia decided to reverse the roles of two of his lead actors. Liang Jingdong, who had originally prepared for the lead role of Cui Mingliang, was asked to trade roles with Wang Hongwei, who ended up giving one of the standout performances in contemporary Chinese cinema as Cui. Perhaps one of the greatest changes between the original conception of the film and the final version is a difference of scale. Ambitious as *Platform* is, Jia's original intention was to make a film that spanned *two* decades, not one, from 1979–99.[49] And although Jia ultimately drew his line of demarcation just after the Tiananmen Square incident of 1989, the historical extension of *Platform*'s philosophy of alienation and cultural change during the 1990s can be seen in *Xiao Wu* and *Unknown Pleasures*.

The last train to Shaoshan

Platform opens with a black screen accompanied by a long, droning, high-pitched whistle. The whistle, which for the time being remains unidentified and seemingly disconnected from any of the action seen in the first shot of the film, resonates with one of the film's central motifs and will, eventually, turn out to be one half of a framing device used by Jia to structure his film.

The opening shot features a group of people standing around gossiping before a theatre performance which they have all gathered to see. The setting is Fenyang, a small- to mid-size city in Shanxi province, and the time is the late 1970s, a few years after the death of Mao; China is just beginning to recover from a decade of political turmoil.

The fashion – drab green and blue tunic jackets and Mao caps – has remained unchanged for the better part of the past thirty years, but change is in the air. In the background a bright diagram with the signage 'Diagram Plan for New Rural Development' is displayed. The image points to a spatial reimagination of the agricultural area around Fenyang, which foretells the massive transformation that will arrive with the Open Door policy and the Four Modernisations.

The promise is of development and change, but as we move inside the performance hall we are privy to an excerpt of one of the

most popularly performed stage dramas of the 1970s, *Train to Shaoshan* (*Huoche xiangzhe Shaoshan pao*). With the introduction of the train motif, we can finally identify the whistle that opened the film as a non-diegetic signifier of the imaginary train about to leave the station – and Jia Zhangke's cinematic train of memories that will take us back to *his* hometown and the era of his youth. With the exception of the scene's first shot, which looks out at the audience from the back of the stage, the entire sequence is shot in one long take from the back of the theatre, with the individual actors barely identifiable. The extreme long shot works to not only blur the distinction between the individual performers on stage, but also indicates that although the imaginary train (made up of a series of small stools the actors scuttle by on) has left the station, the destination is quite distant . . . and perhaps unreachable.

The destination in the play is, of course, Shaoshan, the small town in Hunan province that is famous for being the birthplace of Mao Zedong. The original play depicts a group of passengers from different class and ethnic backgrounds who are united in their eagerness to arrive and break into chorus praising the great Chairman along the way. But, unknown to the players, their imaginary train heading to Mao's hometown – one of the 'holiest' of

Opening scene outside the theatre with the 'Diagram Plan for New Rural Development' in the background

socialist sites in post-1949 China – is in the process of being rerouted under Deng Xiaoping's reform policies and a new breed of 'socialism with Chinese characteristics' which will give priority to the bottom line over the old political line.

From the train we cut to a bus waiting outside the theatre to take the troupe home. The troupe leader Xu (Xi Chuan) goes through a roll call to make sure everyone is aboard. It is through their tardiness that Jia Zhangke first introduces us to the two male protagonists – Zhang Jun and Cui Mingliang. Xu admonishes the latecomers for holding everyone up, criticising them for their 'lack of collective spirit'. When Cui talks back, Xu turns his criticism towards Cui's acting ability, particularly his poor attempt at imitating a train whistle during the evening's performance. The scene is important for delineating a very clear shift from the collective to the individual. During the previous sequence, the emphasis was clearly on a group experience as embodied by both the collective performance and the audience's collective response, laughing and clapping in unison. The extreme long shot did not allow for any individual expressions, emotions, or identities to be transmitted. But once on the bus we are not only given the individual faces (through an extended medium shot), but also their names and, eventually when Cui and Xu start to

Performance of Train to Shaoshan during the opening of Platform

argue, an expression of their personalities; a burgeoning individuality arising out of the collective. The transition displayed between these two early scenes can also be read as a microcosm of the film as a whole, as we are taken on a journey from the collective world of socialist China into a brave new capitalist future where rebellion and western-style individualism is the fashion. But the pathetic attempt at a train whistle sound that Cui Mingliang offers and his admission that he has never even *seen* a train, let alone ridden one, is yet another hint that this journey to modernity may not be an easy one.

As the screen cuts to a blackout and the credits roll (the title 'Platform' finally appears seven minutes and fifty-five seconds into the film) the audio track features a flurry of artificial train sounds produced by the raucous group aboard the bus. The whistling screams announce the beginning of a new journey, as the youngsters embark on a voyage towards an optimistic new future. The sounds reinforce the troupe leader's criticism of Cui Mingliang's poor excuse for a train whistle, collectively mocking him, but they also serve as a narrative bridge back to the opening stage performance.
The whistling cries mark an attempt to transform the beat-up old bus into a modern train speeding off to Shaoshan. Here on display is the stark contrast between the utopian train that unites different classes under communist idealism and the dilapidated bus of the real world where discord, sarcasm and argument rule the day. Jia is already staking out his territory, clearly delineating the almost absurdist rift between the ideal and the real.

As the film progresses, this tension between the ideological beliefs of Maoism come into increasing tension with the burgeoning desires of the individual as the shadow of history silently shifts. Early on in the film narrative, this tension often manifests itself as part of a generational gap. When Cui Mingliang's parents criticise him for wanting bell-bottom trousers (in imitation of his friend Zhang Jun), Cui declares to his mother: 'I'm an art worker, I use my brain.' This attempt to forge an identity distinct from his working-class parents is later reiterated to his father when he is asked to help

To survive, she prostitutes herself on the streets of Paris...

unload logs. Cui responds, 'I'm an art worker, no manual work.'
The same breed of criticism on the part of older characters weary of
the encroaching impact of western liberal thought on young people
can be seen later when Cui's father admonishes his younger son for
reading a comic book adaptation of *Camille*, which depicts the plight
of a prostitute in Paris of all things!

The same traditionalism can be seen in Yin Ruijuan's father in
his criticism of western movies. This clear rift between the generation
of Cui Mingliang and Yin Ruijuan and that of their parents is more
than a generation gap – a more fundamental fissure in politics,
culture and history; between's Mao's China and the new post-
socialist age. As the rapid liberalisation and economic reform that
swept 1980s China continues, it seems that even the old guard can
loose their way. While Cui, Yin and their colleagues all appear at the
vanguard of the new China, as the film progresses (and Deng
Xiaoping's reforms become increasingly pervasive), the older
generation seems to loose the moral direction that was once rooted in
Maoism and lofty socialist ideals. In the second half of the film when
the revamped troupe arrives at another stop on their tour of
developing small towns, the older men in the station office deceive
the girls into giving them a free show. When discovered, all they offer
is a sinister smirk. Most startling, perhaps, is Cui Mingliang's own
father, who once berated his sons for their poor moral character, yet
ends up abandoning his family for a younger second wife. As much of
a portrait of Cui Mingliang's generation's journey and struggle to find
their way, *Platform* is also a critique of how the older generation has

Cui Mingliang demonstrating to his father that he can still squat (and do manual labour)
wearing bell-bottoms and the father criticising his younger son for reading *Camille*

lost their bearings amid a rising tide of reforms that contradict and negate their socialist education and previous life experience under the red flag.

Everyday violence and popular history

Although there are few direct *depictions* of physical violence in *Platform* (one notable exception being Zhang Jun and Cui Mingliang being beaten by thugs at an open-air market while on tour), *narratives* about violence are intricately woven into the fabric of the film. In fact, even during the aforementioned opening shot of the film when a crowd is gathered outside the theatre gossiping before the performance of *Train to Shaoshan*, one of the first items mentioned is the death of a character named Erbao, a topic that is juxtaposed with laughter and inconsequential banter. The matter-of-fact discussion of death foreshadows a series of similar conversations that take place throughout the film. In one such scene Zhong Ping and Yin Ruijuan are enjoying a rare moment together at Zhong's house, but the intimate scene begins with Yin describing how she had just seen a character named Piggy paraded down the street in the back of a truck.

ZHONG PING: What did he do this time?

YIN RUIJUAN: They're going to execute him!

ZHONG PING: Oh, his mother must be really upset!

YIN RUIJUAN: Anyway, the less people like that the better! We should let them die, who cares.

With that, Yin removes her knit work and begins weaving as Zhong Ping turns Yin on to her first cigarette and they gossip about boys and make-up. These and other examples, such as Xu and Cui Mingliang discussing the privatisation of the troupe in a clinic hallway just moments after Zhong Ping goes in for an abortion, all speak to the violence of the everyday that inundates the film and the lives of the characters. The unaffected manner in which violence is repeatedly brought up and brushed aside illustrates the pervasiveness of such violence. Mao once famously wrote 'death happens all the time'. The way in which violence is normalised throughout *Platform* serves as a powerful reminder of the death that huanted the history of the Mao years (through natural disaster, political persecution and famine) and cast a dark shadow over the miraculous reform era and the economic miracles that took place. The price is, of course, not just the deaths themselves, but the way in which it became such a fundamental part of people's everyday lives.

Throughout the film we are presented with numerous examples of the political intermixed with the private, the official intertwined with the quotidian. Film scholar Cui Shuqin discussed one such scene in her article 'Negotiating In-Between':

the loudspeaker first airs a political message – 'construction of a cultural and civilized village' – and then a personal advertisement – 'please come to my household, if anyone needs pork meat.' An official voice of a peasant speaking in standard Mandarin shares the loudspeaker with the voice of a peasant speaking in local dialect; the official political discourse and the commercial pleading of the peasant represent a power negotiation in the soundtrack. Such audio representations not only subordinate a hegemonic authority but also remap social-economic territories so that the local now has a place.[50]

Other similar scenes also serve as an important facet of *Platform*'s historicisation as the film subtly juxtaposes major historical events with private events in the characters' lives. These scenes provide a historical context for the story and collectively map out a timeline, but often Jia also uses such juxtapositions to an ironic effect. When Zhang Jun and Zhong Ping arrive at the Wenzhou Hair Salon for Zhong to get her first perm they do so in the middle of a street parade promoting the one-child policy and the importance of family planning. The parade serves as a historical marker, telling the viewer that it is 1979, the year the policy was implemented, but just a few scenes later when Zhang Jun and Zhong Ping are seen standing outside a nearby abortion clinic, Jia's melancholic irony is powerfully felt.

These silent juxtapositions of the historical with the personal can be seen throughout Jia's work. In *Xiao Wu*, just as the protagonist is exiled from his family we hear an announcement of the reunification of Hong Kong with China. Once again the juxtaposition is not merely to provide a historical context (in this case 1997), but also to highlight the irony of a newly unified country with a newly destroyed family (which is, after all, the basis of the nation in traditional Confucian thought). In *Platform*, another such example occurs when the thirty-fifth anniversary of the founding of the PRC (1984) is announced over a radio broadcast as Zhong Ping slaps Zhang Jun and stamps into the clinic operating room to have her abortion. Here the birthday of the nation is sarcastically matched with the death of Zhong's unborn child. Towards the end of the film a loudspeaker announcement issues a list of criminals wanted by the government (a cryptic reference to the crackdown in the wake of the 1989 student demonstrations) which coincides with the end of Cui Mingliang's idealistic wanderings and his settling down into a stable family. But once again, Jia Zhangke cannot help but put an ironic twist on history. In a tone typical of official state announcements, a female voice reads off the list of suspects: 'Yu Lik Wai, twenty-four, male, born in Guangdong province, a native of Zhongshan county, 5.58 feet. He has a stong Cantonese accent and is fluent in French.' Yu is, of course, not a student activist, but Jia's Hong Kong cinematographer. In a comic self-referential move, Jia has also touched on the very real predicament that he and fellow independent film-makers faced as 'illegal' or 'underground' artists.

But most often in *Platform*, history is conveyed not through references to large-scale historical incidents like the implementation of the one-child policy (1979), the Sino-British Joint Talks (1984), or the Tiananmen Square massacre (1989), but rather through subtle changes in pop culture; fashion, television, films, dance and, especially, popular music. Over the course of the film, we see the gradual evolution of popular fashion from the unisex tunic jackets and overcoats ubiquitous during the Mao era to the tank tops, jogging trousers and athletic wear that became all the rage in the early to mid-1980s and later from leather jackets and blue jeans to sports jackets and slacks. Jia utilises fashion to convey not only the passage of time, but the personal trajectory of his characters as they move through stages of rebellion, self-discovery and, ultimately, responsibility. The true genius of *Platform*'s fashion sensibility lies in its portrayals of transition phases, such as Cui Mingliang wearing his home-made bell-bottoms with his Mao jacket. McGrath has also observed how,

the film eschews easily identified, monolithic changes in the characters' dress and hairstyles as the narrative (and decade) progresses; rather than all characters' transparently signifying the transition, say, from 1979 to the early 1980s, some characters suddenly appear with permed hair or in track suits, while others retain the earlier styles of the Mao era, reflecting the multiple temporal frames of reference that actually coexist at any particular historical moment.[51]

Such hybrid fashions provide subtle yet consistent visual markers of the radical historical changes taking place, and often tell of the tensions and contradictions implicit within.

Another way in which *Platform* reveals the tensions at play within this period of historical change is through a series of dance routines, which transition from ballet and Spanish dance to disco and slam-dancing. Historical tension is revealed not just through the transition between different dance styles as the film progresses, but also through the stark clash between the various dance routines and the environment in which they take place. These sequences include Zhong Ping with her new perm and a red rose clenched between her teeth dancing a tango before the portrait of Chairman Mao in the troupe meeting room, the entire troupe rocking out to the modern disco-rock of Zhang Di's 'Genghis Khan' ('Chengji Sihan') in Zhong Ping's father's small, dark, dilapidated workshop, or a uniformed Yin Ruijuan dancing a beautiful freestyle routine to Su Rui's 'If It's True' ('Shifou') in the middle of an empty tax office. Like Cui wearing his 'fashionable' bell-bottoms with an old Mao jacket, these sequences unveil the clash between a higher cultural world that the characters' aspire to and the environment they remain trapped within. Through such moments, Jia displays glimpses of his humour, but beyond the laughter that such radical juxtapositions often inspire also lies a deep melancholy. For these are portraits of people trying use art, fashion and dance to transcend their environment, but as the film ultimately reveals, when the walls are high such transcendence can be difficult to achieve.

As is also the case with many of Jia Zhangke's other films, popular music often proves to be the single most powerful tool to not only signal social change and historical transition, but also to simultaneously serve as an internal commentary on the action unfolding on-screen. From the odes to Chairman Mao featured in the opening stage performance of *Train to Shaoshan* to the Bollywood classic 'Awara Hoon' or from the soothing sounds of Teresa Teng's 'Coffee and Wine' ('Meijiu jia kafei') coming over an illegal short-wave radio broadcast from Taiwan to the rise of China's own local rock and pop superstars such as Zhang Di, *Platform* subtly weaves these dramatic changes in music culture into the film's narrative. While similar changes in pop music occurred over the course of fifty years in the west, here we witness equally sweeping changes compacted into the span of just a single decade as the film moves from opera and socialist anthems to love ballads and rock 'n' roll.

Perhaps the single most important song to appear in the film is the piece that inspired the title, 'Platform' ('Zhantai'). Originally performed by Zhang Xing, a member of China's first generation of bona-fide rockstars, 'Platform' spoke to a lost and alienated generation.

> The long and empty platform
> The wait seems never ending
> The long box cars are carrying my short-lived love
> The long and empty platform
> Lonely, we can only wait
> All my love is out-bound
> Nothing on the in-bound train

Zhang Xing inspired young people throughout China, not only with his pioneering music, but also the cosmopolitan image he represented with 'his impeccably tailored suit, slicked-back hair, and stylish dark glasses'.[52] As one-time sideman to the pop icon Dennis Rea remarked, 'By anything-goes Western standards, Zhang Xing's repertoire of revved-up Taiwan and Hong Kong pop ballads was laughably tame, but his swoony love songs provided the ultimate in titillation to a public bored with bland socialist entertainment.'[53] The message of Zhang's music also had a deep effect on Jia Zhangke who features the song twice in the film, first in a desolate area where the troupe's truck has broken down when Cui Mingliang puts one of Zhang Xing's cassette tapes into the dashboard stereo (a scene described in more detail later), and later when Cui himself covers the song with the reconstituted version of the troupe in a tent to a rowdy audience. On several occasions Jia has recalled the impact 'Platform' had on him as a young man growing up in Fenyang:

'Platform' is a song from the mid-eighties that was especially popular among young people; it was also the very first rock-and-roll song I ever heard. The lyrics describe someone waiting on a platform for the arrival of his lover, expressing a mood of expectation. For me, that song represents a key to unlock my memories of the eighties. The 'Platform' is a place from which one sets out, but also returns to. The 'Platform' is related to the journey; I always loved the title of that song which captures the exhaustion and sadness of life.[54]

As Jason McGrath has commented, 'the song captures both the promise of an approaching modernity and the frustration of waiting endlessly for it in an inconsequential (yet therefore representative) small city in China's hinterland'.[55] In many ways, 'Platform' serves as the spiritual heart of the film, hinting at an imaginary station, where the characters await a dream train to take them away to the outside world. But, as the film ultimately reveals, that imaginary platform is an illusive destination.

Between the ruins of socialism and the throes of reform

In many ways, *Platform* is a cinematic tone poem on historical change, a meditation on how seemingly subtle shifts in pop culture, politics and economics can exert transformative powers on individuals on a scale that is nothing short of epic.[56] The key message is that the seemingly subtle shifts are actually anything but subtle, instead constituting a complete reimagination of society and culture. The shift from socialism to capitalism, China to the west, and from public to the private are displayed in *Platform* via a constantly shifting matrix of radical juxtapositions that tease out the pervasive changes taking place. In this context it seems fitting that Jia highlights

Han Aihua and Zhang Jun stroll past a 1977 political slogan in the hand of Hua Guofeng

the presence of the transitional political figurehead of Hua Guofeng (Mao's chosen successor who was ultimately ousted by Deng Xiaoping), who appears in the film via radio broadcasts and slogans on walls. Hua is a figure that is largely forgotten and written out of many official PRC histories, which prefer a 'cleaner' direct lineage from Mao to Deng. Just as Hua is an ephemeral, almost invisible, figure, *Platform* seems to be most keenly interested not in *the event* but in the transitory moment between historical events – the kinds of everyday occurrences that are usually overlooked not only by 'history' but even by 'cinema', with its prejudice towards 'drama' and 'action'. As a portrait of history in transition and lives in transit, *Platform* retrieves everyday moments and experiences, examining the plight of individuals caught in the throes of historical change.

Jia's visual language for displaying such transition is often filled with a combination of hope and sadness and, often, irony. In one scene, Eryong, Zhang Jun and Cui Mingliang, piled onto a single bicycle, arrive to meet Zhong Ping and Yin Ruijuan, who are waiting for them outside a theatre. Upon arrival, Zhang Jun shows off his brand-new bell-bottom trousers before the group of friends go

Zhang Jun (second from left) shows off his bell-bottom trousers to Zhong Ping and Yin Ruijian (foreground) and Eryong (centre) and Cui Mingliang (right) look on. The faded political slogan in the background bears the name of Marx

in to see a 'foreign film'. All the while, however, the spectre of Marx looms in the background via a fading political slogan from the not-so-distant past and the grey soviet-style architecture that frames the scene.

Throughout the 1980s, these two realms would repeatedly negotiate and renegotiate the boundaries and limitations between conservatism and liberalism, socialism and capitalism. *Platform* is not about a simple transition, but the awkwardness and contradictions implicit within that transition. Other examples of this can be seen in several pairs of scenes that take place in radically different spaces. One such couplet takes place alternately in the beauty salon and the troupe meeting room with the action centred around Zhong Ping's new perm – a certain signpost of the new fashion waves storming small-town Fenyang. The pair of scenes effectively map out the movement from one space to the other, from the perm's natural setting of the hair salon to the troupe meeting room, where Zhong's sudden appearance takes on an almost grotesque characteristic as it is placed amid a sterile environment of party rhetoric and cadres wearing Mao jackets. Immediately, the new perm becomes the butt of the troupe leader Xu's sarcastic jokes. Also, one can see the transition illustrated through the set design and various props, including the two portraits that dominate the respective scenes – a fashionable female model with a perm versus a classic portrait of the dear leader Chairman Mao, rendered askew by the camera angle.

Zhang Jun and Zhong Ping inside the Wenzhou Hair Salon and the troupe meeting chaired by Xu (second from left)

It is not just the transition between these two shots that Jia uses to illustrate change and historical tensions, it is also the internal dynamics *within* each that further tease out the pressures playing out. While the internal world of the Wenzhou Hair Salon seems to be a self-contained world of liberalism and openness, the cadre smoking in centre frame and the state-sponsored parade promoting the one-child policy going on just outside speak otherwise. And just as the troupe meeting room appears to be an example of a conservative socialist space, the sudden infiltration of Zhong Ping with her 'western-style permanent wave' provides a telling signpost of the instability of 'orthodox socialism'.

These negotiations represent a fundamental part of the film's *mise en scène*, aesthetic vision, as well as the overarching philosophy of the work.

If we are to break the settings of various scenes in the film into official spaces (i.e. the meeting room of the Cultural Troupe) and private or unofficial spaces (i.e. the Wenzhou Hair Salon), we consistently see the infiltration of elements from one space into the other. This cross-pollination of influences is indicative of a much larger negotiation that is being carried on between China and the west, socialism and capitalism, the public and the private, the state and the individual. Jia Zhangke's presentation of this dialectic is never forced and seems to naturally unfold with the story, but closer scrutiny reveals this tension as a meticulously designed facet of his cinematic vision.

Another such example occurs early on when several of the protagonists meet outside a local theatre to catch an afternoon screening of the classic Indian film *Awāra* (1951).[57] But here in this dimly lit non-official space where a rambunctious audience watches the protagonist (a petty thief) sing 'Awara Hoon' ('I am a Tramp') an interruption occurs as an announcement breaks out, 'Yin Ruijuan of the Cultural Team! There is someone here to see you!' That someone is Ruijuan's father, a policeman (played by Liang Yonghao, who also played Hao, the policeman, in *Xiao Wu*) who has come to check up

on his daughter and discourage her from watching foreign films and
hanging around with the wrong crowd (including Cui Mingliang
whom Yin's father disapproves of). Cui Shuqin has observed how the
loudspeaker bears a 'violence . . ., recalling the socialist era,
suppresses other sounds and the everyday life of the people'.[58]
As Ruijuan exits the theatre and appears in the lobby, we are
suddenly transported to a most public space, brightly lit and adorned
by hanging portraits of Lenin and Stalin. A third portrait of 'Young
Mao' lies on a stand directly between Ruijuan and her father – a
powerful metaphor for the ideological rift that keeps father and
daughter separated. The radical separation of these two spaces is
further enhanced by a hint of violence marked by a blatant display
the state's power to discipline and punish, as evidenced by the group
of young men forced to squat against the wall by Ruijuan's father.
But here in this space stamped with all of the signifiers of power and
the state, as Ruijuan's father criticises her for exposing herself to the
corruptive forces of 'foreign films', we hear the music to 'Awara
Hoon' continually bleeding into the soundtrack. Creeping in
whenever the door opens, the music provides an ironic teasing
commentary on the action at hand, undermining the power of the
father and further conflating the division between the official and the
non-official.

The song 'Awara Hoon' proves most illustrative when one
listens to the actual lyrics:

Interior and exterior: Raj Kapoor's *Awāra* on-screen and Yin Ruijuan and her father
in the cinema lobby

I'm a tramp, I'm a tramp
Whether I'm rising or falling, I'm always a star
I have no family, no home
I have no one who loves me
I don't have a lover waiting for me across the river
For me the city is an empty city, the unknown path is all I love
I'm not rich, I'd rather stay a pauper
But the songs I sing are merry songs
My heart is full of wounds, but my eyes are always full of smiles
Oh, this world! In this world perhaps I'm doomed![59]

In *Awāra* the song appears during a fast-paced sequence immediately after the protagonist Raj (portrayed by director Raj Kapoor) is released from prison and we see the thief quickly revert back to his old ways. As Raj sings (or rather lip-syncs the song, the original was sung by Mukesh), we witness him lifting a pocket watch, chased by a victim in fast-motion Chaplin style, stealing a bicycle and hopping on a moving trolley before being ejected by the disapproving passengers. The song also follows Raj on a journey that takes him from the urban centre of town to the dilapidated slums outside of town, where his journey ends. At the heart of his song is his admission of his identity as an 'awāra', a rogue, tramp, or drifter. The song and accompanying sequence from *Awāra* appear in *Platform* just as Cui Mingliang is being set up to lose his own love and bid farewell to his family as he sets out on his own journey as a rogue drifter with the remnants of the once state-sponsored song and dance troupe. Given the theme and content of the song – a playful ode to the drifter – it is doubly significant that it is the official discourse of a policeman, Yin Ruijuan's father, that interrupts the song. This disturbance foreshadows the actual departure of the troupe several scenes later when Yin Ruijuan, who was originally set to accompany Cui and the troupe on their adventures, is forced to stay behind to care for her father who has suddenly fallen ill.

The appropriation of Raj Kapoor's *Awāra* is also illustrative in terms of the internal commentary the film seems to project on Jia's own work. Audiences familiar with Jia Zhangke's oeuvre will immediately think back to *Xiao Wu*, another tale of a pickpocket that also ends with the protagonist shackled behind bars. But while the climax in *Awāra* leaves the pickpocket with real hope for redemption – as he goes to prison his lover vows to wait for him, he wins acceptance from his long-estranged father and Raj himself promises to fulfil his birthright by studying to become 'a lawyer, a magistrate and then a judge' – these are all luxuries denied Xiao Wu who is abandoned by his lover and disowned by his family. But of more immediate relevance to *Platform* is *Awāra*'s central theme of fate and identity as the protagonist struggles to overcome a life of crime (the path laid out for him by a scheming gangster) in order to pursue a path of goodness serving the law (the path originally planned for him by his father, a renowned judge). A similar theme plays out in *Platform* as Cui Mingliang continually attempts to change his fate while his parents insist on his knowing his proper place.

Such a conflict is demonstrated most clearly in the aforementioned bell-bottom scene, where Cui insists he is an 'art worker' while his father reminds him of the impracticality of 'peasants' doing manual labour wearing tight bell-bottoms. While Cui attempts to use culture to rise above the limitations of his environment, his circumstances continually bring him back down – we see him doing manual labour at the troupe's headquarters just a few scenes later. As Cui and his colleagues place shards of broken glass along the tops of the exterior walls to deter thieves (and all the Xiao Wus that might be prowling about), we are also privy to another signpost of China in transition – as the shift towards capitalism brings with it an increasing lag between the haves and have-nots and a steep rise in petty crime. It is scenes like this, in concert with the film's masterful conclusion, that demonstrate the heavy weights attached to the romantic dreams of Cui's youth and China's modernisation project.

Of platforms and walls

One of the key sites during the first half of *Platform* is the old city wall, which almost becomes a character of its own with its arched gateways, steep rail-less staircases and protruding bastions. The wall also conjures memories of the dilapidated city wall appearing at the opening of the classic film *Spring in a Small Town* (*Xiaocheng zhi chun*) (1948), which also takes place during a period of massive historical change as China moves from the ruins of war into a new era. In *Platform*, the city wall works as a separate space where Zhang Jun, Cui Mingliang and the others congregate, create mischief, sing songs and assert their identity. Jia exploits the stunning angles and desolate atmosphere of the wall most effectively during a series of encounters that take place there between Cui Mingliang and Yin Ruijuan. The trio of key scenes between the two that take place around the old Fenyang city wall display Jia's masterful use of *mise en scène* to portray the transformation of his characters' relationship. And although each sequence is shot at the same site with the same cast, Jia's use of different angles, camera distances and shot lengths brilliantly displays his creative use of variations in editing and cinematography to accentuate emotional content.

The first scene in the series occurs shortly after the screening of *Awāra* at the local theatre. Dusk is approaching on a winter day and Cui and Yin meet atop the wall where they speak briefly before heading down below to avoid the scrutiny of Yin's father. Although he is no longer present, like in the movie theatre, the father

The first encounter atop the city wall and the couple continuing their conversation below

once again becomes a hindrance to Cui and Yin's union.
The conversation seems a bit more promising as they discuss the smooth development of Zhong Ping and Zhang Jun's relationship, at least until Cui brings up Yin's father yet again:

CUI MINGLIANG: Your Dad's really something.

YIN RUIJUAN: What do you mean?

CUI MINGLIANG: He's like a KGB agent.

YIN RUIJUAN: Don't say that, he's my dad. Since Mum died, he's taken care of me.

CUI MINGLIANG: But he's like a military dictator!

YIN RUIJUAN: Don't say that!

Although they descend the wall to escape from the gaze of the father, his shadow looms and Cui wages a fruitless oedipal revolt; the conversation deteriorates further. The coldness of the scene is enhanced by the blanket of snow and overcast sky, which further accentuate the physical and emotional distance of the couple. As the conversation dies down, Cui remains silent, but he throws a match on the ground which ignites a medium-size fire. The flame, which can be seen as a physical representation of Cui's temper, blazes out of control as Yin tells of her family's attempt to set her up with a dentist. Nelson Yu Lik Wai's camera observes the scene from a cool distance, pulling back from a medium long shot atop the wall to an extreme long shot when Cui and Yin descend to speak in private. Instead of offering a series of conventional close-ups as their talk grows more uncomfortable, the camera's distance further accentuates the emotional distance between the would-be lovers.

In contrast to the film's liberal use of popular music, use of Yoshihiro Hanno's score is extremely restrained, featured only three times in the film.[60] It is only during the last few seconds of this first scene at the city wall – some twenty minutes into the film – that Yoshihiro Hanno's non-diagetic score is first heard. The fifteen-second theme appears just as the flames are burning out of control and it can be seen as a powerful accent to mark the development of Cui and Yin's relationship. The same musical theme will appear again ninety minutes into the film, after the troupe sees a train for the first time. Once again, the melancholic theme is accompanied by fire as Cui lights a patch of diesel fuel on the ground and stares at the flames, lost in deep thought – the burning fire an apparent symbol of his longing for Yin Ruijuan. The score returns for a third and final time at the end of the film as Cui and Yin silently sit in her apartment, marking their final reunion. In this final example the early embers that blaze at the base of the city wall and the raging flames seen in the middle of the film are all but extinguished, their only remnant being the feeble cigarette in Cui's hand – a telling commentary on fading passion, retreating ideals and doused dreams. Although they are finally together, the elegiac nature of the score reminds us that the final union is not entirely celebratory.

The second meeting between Cui and Yin atop the city wall occurs some thirty scenes later. And although this time the encounter is presented with an extended medium shot, here the physicality of the wall itself, which continually separates the characters, takes the place of camera distance as the primary cinematic tool to visually highlight their estrangement. Their repeated exchange of places, with one half of the pair consistently obscured by the wall in the foreground, complements their shifting stances as each is put on the defensive. This encounter also marks the first time in the film that Cui offers the closest example of an attempt to formalise their

Trading places: Yin Ruijuan and Cui Mingliang during their second meeting atop the wall

relationship. With his back literally against the wall, Cui asks: 'Yesterday I was talking to this guy and at the end of our conversation he asked me a question. He asked if Yin Ruijuan was my girlfriend. What do you say?' Cui's indirect question is brushed aside by Yin's casual response, 'How could some people be so nosy?' When Cui presses her that he too would like to know, Yin answers, 'I don't know.' Cui quickly leaves, slowly riding off on his bicycle as Yin straggles behind him walking. While the visual separation between the two characters (they are almost never seen in the same shot during the conversation) is emphasised throughout the sequence, audiences observe the subtle evolution of their relationship from their first encounter on the wall. Although the setting is the same, the snow has now melted, afternoon light has replaced the dusk, and Cui has finally mustered the courage to actually discuss the nature of their hazy relationship.

In the final city wall encounter between Cui Mingliang and Yin Ruijuan we are presented with the couple at the base of the wall under an arched gateway. Cui had cut his hand in a previous scene just as Zhong Ping encouraged him to talk to Yin Ruijuan about his feelings for her – the self-inflicted injury a portent of what is to come when he finally opens up. The circle of sunlight that surrounds Cui as he reveals his feelings serves as a spotlight highlighting his vulnerability, which is further accented by his wounded hand, which now appears bandaged. Yin, on the other hand, remains partially obscured in the shadows as she rejects Cui, explaining how her father

Cui and Yin at the base of the wall and Cui alone atop the wall a few scenes later

never approved of him and she herself also has doubts about their compatibility. References to Yin Ruijuan's father during all three encounters atop the wall are significant as they demonstrate the strong association between the traditional authority, both patriarchal (as Yin Ruijuan's father) and legal (as a policeman), that the father carries. Through these sequences, the symbolic place of the father collapses into the wall itself, which is, after all, built to keep people out, just as he attempts to keep Cui out of his daughter's life. As Xiaoping Lin has observed, 'the thick, gloomy, and self-contained city wall' is clearly a 'metaphorical allusion to the oppressive patriarchal authorities'.[61] Their meeting ends with a broken Cui Mingliang ascending the stairway to the top of the wall and a distraught Yin Ruijuan pacing aimlessly along the bottom of the wall. Suddenly an announcement comes over a loudspeaker from the nearby bus station, 'Bus 27 to Songjiachuan is ready to depart!' The seemingly random example of ambient noise bleeding into the soundtrack of these characters' lives breaks the silence and foreshadows the imminent departure of Cui. Now severed from his true love, he will prepare to embark on a new journey.

Stubborn, immovable and traditional, the wall serves as a powerful metaphor for the seeming impossibility of their relationship. A few scenes later, we see Cui alone atop the wall; he gazes out towards Yin Ruijuan's apartment, which lies just across the way. This marks an inversion of the first encounter on the wall, which began with Cui alone atop the wall in winter, before meeting up with Yin and descending together. This third and final sequence begins at the base of the wall and concludes with Cui back at the top. Jia creates a neat structural symmetry from this trio of encounters that visually conveys the tension and (apparent) destruction of the pair's fragile relationship.

Jia Zhangke adds an ironic footnote to the scene by immediately juxtaposing Cui's romantic loss with his father's infidelities. Just as a broken-hearted Cui Mingliang returns home having failed at love, his mother reveals details that imply her husband has been carrying on a secret affair. The conservative father who once criticised his sons for wearing bell-bottom trousers and reading *Camille* now reinvents himself as the most liberal and progressive one in the family – and romantically the most successful.

The city wall is not just a meeting place for the would-be lovers' rendezvous, but carries much broader meaning in the context of *Platform*'s other themes of movement. As a symbol of staunch immobility, protection from the outside and tradition, the wall is what separates the characters from their 'hometown' and the outside world. Thus the ancient city wall stands as the direct antithesis to the train motif that continually recurs and is alluded to in the film's title. After his rejection by Yin Ruijuan, Cui ascends the wall where he teeters on the brink of Fenyang and the outside world, wavering, and soon he will set out to see the wide world that lies beyond.

The drive towards the outside world is not a sudden shift driven simply by Cui's rejection, but the natural development in a series of cultural, social and economic changes that have been gradually taking place throughout the film. This proclivity towards the fashions, tastes, experiences of that which lies beyond the walls of Fenyang is perhaps best exemplified not by Cui Mingliang, but his friend and fellow 'art worker', Zhang Jun. Zhang's keen interest and fascination with the cosmopolitan world lurking beyond the reality of his everyday life in Shanxi is continually highlighted and its evolution also becomes a key force impacting the lives of those around him, as they too increasingly fall under the spell of his big-city dreams.

Zhang Jun's transformation can be seen from the very beginning of the film, as embodied by his knowledge and interest in urban popular culture partially attributed to his family ties in Guangzhou. He appears mesmerised as he listens to his friend Eryong's stories about pickpockets in big cities using razorblades to cut victims' pockets open to lift their wallets. He is the first one in Fenyang to own a pair of bell-bottom trousers, a gift from his auntie in Guangzhou. When Deng Xiaoping first instituted his economic reform policies, the plan called for a select minority to prosper first. In most cases, the first to bear the riches of Deng's reforms were those in coastal port cities, such as Guangzhou, Shanghai and Wenzhou and it was often from these centres that the latest fashions from Hong Kong, Taiwan and overseas were adapted and spread. Almost immediately, Cui Mingliang has his mother make him his very own pair of bell-bottom trousers – a potent display of the rapid imitation and dissemination of popular fashions.

Zhang is also at the vanguard when it comes to liberalised views on dating and sexuality. While Cui Mingliang still struggles to win the affections of Yin Ruijuan, Zhang already has a steady relationship with Zhong Ping. We should also not forget that when Zhong Ping first gets her perm – a haircut that shakes up the Fenyang song and dance troupe, even inspiring the addition of a new Spanish tango to the performance repertoire – it is actually Zhang Jun that pressures her into getting the perm. As her boyfriend, Zhong Ping's perm is as much a step in *his* road to modernity as it is to hers. Zhang takes Zhong to the Wenzhou Hair Salon, where he excitedly talks to the hairdresser about Wenzhou and Guangzhou. (The actual inspiration for the perm can be seen a few scenes earlier when Zhang flirts with another girl, Han Aihua, that already has a perm and he quickly encourages Zhong Ping to get a similar haircut.) During a later conversation with Yin Ruijuan, Zhong also admits she has begun wearing eye make-up for Zhang Jun as well.

But Zhang Jun's true odyssey begins when he leaves Fenyang to visit his auntie in Guangzhou. While away, he sends a postcard to his friend:

> Mingliang:
>
> It's wonderful to see the dazzling world!
>
> > Your friend,
> > Zhang Jun, May 1981

The postcard features a colour aerial view of the city of Guangzhou and Jia Zhangke highlights the importance of the postcard for Cui Mingliang by presenting close-up images of both the front and back of the card – one of the only close-ups in the entire film.

The postcard represents a romanticised version of the world outside Fenyang, providing hope for Cui as he is stuck living with his parents in a provincial small town. Soon, Zhang Jun returns from his adventure bearing the fruits of big-city life. Decked out in a fashionable shirt with Japanese script, sunglasses and carrying a portable cassette boom-box, Zhang immediately becomes the centre of attention. Cui jokingly calls him a 'pseudo-foreign devil' and the troupe members surround him, inundating him with questions about his experiences as the latest pop hits blare out of his boom-box. In the process of bearing newfound dreams of change to the other characters, Zhang Jun's cosmopolitan experiences also effectively reframe traditional notions of the hometown. Through this process, the hometown is no longer the romanticised site of longing, but rather a site from which one longs to escape.

It is not long after Zhang Jun's triumphant return to Fenyang that talk of the song and dance troupe's privatisation begins to heat up. The first mention of the impending privatisation takes place between Xu and Cui in the lobby of a women's clinic as Zhong Ping goes in to have an abortion. The natural dialogue and matter-of-fact exchange conceals the film's implied juxtaposition of Zhong's abortion with privatisation – the state aborting its traditional responsibilities, severing the umbilical cord that ties it to countless

Zhang Jun's message to Cui Mingliang, flip side of the postcard from Guangzhou former industries, factories and work units. A clear signpost of the massive infrastructural changes taking place within Chinese society, the troupe's handover also indicates a change in leadership from Xu, the former educated youth intent on using Maoist doctrines of self-criticism and ideological 'correctness' to instruct and lead, to Song Yongping, the pragmatic electrician who buys out the troupe, much to the surprise of its members. One of the first steps to make the transition from a state-subsidised work unit to a private enterprise is to generate profit by taking the troupe on the road. Zhang Jun, Zhong Ping, Cui Mingliang and many of the other original members all decide to go, Yin Ruijuan, however, opts to stay behind in order to care for her ailing father – once again, the father serves as the barrier separating the couple. In a powerful image emphasising her isolation, Yin stares out from her apartment balcony in silence, the city wall in the background sealing her in.

As the troupe sets out, their dumpy tractor drives past the same dilapidated wall seen earlier outside the theatre. The only characters immediately recognisable on the large fading political slogan are *Makesi* – the Chinese transliteration of Marx. As the tractor pulls away, Cui gazes teary-eyed into the distance, perhaps secretly hoping

Yin Ruijuan staring out at the wall looming in the distance from her apartment front balcony

that Yin Ruijuan might miraculously appear to see him off.
Meanwhile, the other troupe members piled into the trailer bed of the
tractor sing 'Goodbye friends, goodbye, friends . . .'. This is not just a
farewell to Fenyang and the friends and family of their hometown,
but a farewell to the ideologies of yesterday. As Marx, Mao and the
spectres of socialism literally fade into the distance, the newly
privatised song and dance troupe, now cut off from the state,
embarks on a bold new mission into the future.

As the tractor pulls through the city gate and past the wall,
Jia Zhangke offers us the very first point-of-view shot in the film.
The dynamic scenes of the quickly retreating city stand in stark
contrast to the fixed shots and slow pans of the rest of the film.
The implied perspective is that of Cui Mingliang as he gazes back
from the bed of the truck – and, for the very first time, time seems to
quicken.[62] Significantly, it is only when the characters leave their
hometown that we finally see it through their eyes. With their
departure, however, the train implied by the film's title still fails to
appear. With no railway station in Fenyang, Cui's departure is not via
train, just as the recently privatised song and dance troupe fails to
venture to the glamorous southern cities of Guangzhou or Fuzhou,
which inspire their dreams. Instead, the troupe's first stop is a

Point-of-view shot as the tractor pulls out of the city gate and away from Fenyang neighbouring rural town just outside of Fenyang reliant on coalmining.

The troupe sets up on an old, dilapidated outdoor theatre stage, while Song Yongping negotiates with the local town heads. It is here that Cui Mingliang encounters his cousin Sanming (played by the director's own cousin, Han Sanming) – a meeting that brings Cui and the troupe face to face with the realities of backwardness, poverty and exploitation. Cui, who initially does not recognise Sanming, who has grown a beard since their last meeting, is struck by his cousin's transformation. The encounter is reminiscent of the famous meeting between the narrator and Runtu in Lu Xun's masterful short story 'My Old Home', a seminal text exploring the rift between nostalgic romanticisation and the bleak reality of home. Having been away from home for many years, the educated narrator returns to the place of his upbringing to encounter his childhood playmate Runtu, now a middle-aged, illiterate peasant.

I knew at a glance that this was Runtu, it was not the Runtu I remembered. He had grown to twice his former size. His round face, once crimson, had become sallow and acquired deep lines and wrinkles; his eyes too had become like his father's, the rims swollen and red, a feature common to most peasants who work by the sea and are exposed all day to the wind from the ocean. He wore a shabby felt cap and just one very thin padded jacket, with the result that he was shivering from head to foot. He carried a paper package and a long pipe, nor was his hand the plump red hand I remembered, but coarse and clumsy and chapped, like the bark of a pine tree.[63]

The encounter between Lu Xun's narrator and Runtu bears a strong resemblance to the awkward reunion between Cui Mingliang and Sanming: not only for the formalistic similarities of the meeting between former childhood playmates now of two distinct social classes, the silence and inability to articulate their experience which marks both Runtu and Sanming, but most of all for the deep sense of tragedy, inequality and sadness that affects both protagonists. For the majority of Chinese viewers seeing *Platform* (primarily urban audiences) and virtually all foreign audiences, the vision of Fenyang projected on-screen already feels provincial and backward, but here Jia Zhangke reminds us there are realities far more sobering, fates far more tragic.

The dark realities of rural China are reinforced not just through Sanming's silent gazes and numb responses, but through a series of scenes that paint a portrait of desperation and exploitation. Sanming's mother explains the family's predicament when it comes to finding a wife for Sanming and providing continued support for their daughter's tuition, 'The only work here is in the fields and in the mines . . . we're almost starving.' And later when Sanming goes to sign up for a new job at a local coalmine, the crude mine boss makes his stance all too clear, 'We're not responsible for anything.' Coming from a system where the state was responsible for *everything*, providing family housing, healthcare and other benefits under the 'iron rice-bowl' of the socialist system, the new reality of capitalist exploitation is spelled out in the contract that Sanming must sign before he is allowed to work:

Contract: 1: Life and death are questions of fate. I'm willing to work in Gao's mine. Management accepts no blame for accidents. 2: In cases of death or accident the mine offers 500 yuan compensation to families. 3: Daily wage is 10 yuan.

The other indictment comes via Yu Lik Wai's camera as it slowly pans over the dry, dark, parched land, presenting the environment itself as another factor contributing to the oppression of the countryside. Here, Jia Zhangke returns to the same mountainous landscape that inspired him in *Yellow Earth* (which was shot in neighbouring Shaanxi) to present a similarly powerful portrait of peasant strife – the main difference being that Chen's film was set in the 1940s, before the communist victory, and Jia's is set in the 1980s,

amid the economic miracles taking place throughout China and after four decades of communist rule.

From Sanming's village (and most likely the original hometown of Cui Mingliang's family), the troupe ventures on across various locations in Shanxi and northern China, including Shaanxi and Inner Mongolia. We gradually witness the transformation of the company, as old members such as Zhong Ping break away and new members such as the identical twins Li Xiaojuan and Li Xiaoe, who become the troupe's new showcase dancers, join up. With these changes also comes the replacement of traditional instruments such as the accordion, *erhu* and violin with electric guitar, electric bass, keyboards and western-style drum kit, a shift that is complemented by a new repertoire of Chinese pop-rock hits. Eventually the former Fenyang County Rural Cultural Work Team is renamed the Shenzhen Allstars Rock and Breakdance Electronic Band. While Shenzhen in the mid- to late 1980s was but a second-rate copy of Hong Kong, for the rest of China it was still very much cutting edge.

The appropriation of Shenzhen – the instant city across the Pearl River delta that mushroomed into prosperity thanks to Deng Xiaoping's economic policies – as the fictitious hometown of the troupe speaks not only to the group's cosmopolitan dreams, but also

Sanming and Cui Mingliang against the forbidding landscape of hills and mines demonstrates Song Yongping's savvy marketing strategy that capitalises on Shenzhen as the new epicentre of 'urban cool'. Eventually, as Cui Shuqin has noted, the troupe even goes so far as to 'lure an audience with announcements from the loudspeaker that its performers are "stars from the United States and Singapore" '.[64] But while the troupe brands itself with a name symbolic of prosperity and economic revitalisation and identifies its members as bearers of global modernity, there are no miracles awaiting the group as they trudge through the underbelly of China, performing in makeshift tents or on the open bed of their transport truck. Zhang Jun, Cui Mingliang and the rest of the group tour some of north China's most impoverished areas and traverse some of the country's harshest terrain.

Eventually, the long-awaited train suggested in the film's title does appear, but there is no 'platform' and the train never stops. With their truck broken down in the middle of a desolate valley, Cui sits in the cab and pops in a cassette tape of Zhang Xing's 'Platform'. As the music plays, the sound of an approaching train breaks out and the troupe races to the tracks to witness the spectacle. As they arrive beside the tracks, the slow-moving freight train has already chugged past and Cui Mingliang, Zhang Jun, Zhong Ping and the others scream out as it moves into the distance. Their cries seem to hint at a mixture of elation and desolation and refer back to the humoured cries that appear at the beginning of the film during the title sequence. This is the only time a train appears in the film and it takes them nowhere. For Jia, for whom 'the train stands for hope and the future',[65] this relative absence is telling indeed.

> The long and empty platform
> The wait seems never ending.

The train of dreams that leads to Shenzhen, Hong Kong and beyond never arrives in *Platform*. And the characters' incessant searching never seems to bring them to that imaginary destination. But that is because Cui Mingliang, Zhang Jun, Eryong, Zhong Ping,

Yin Ruijuan and the rest of the troupe are not aboard the train, but left on the platform waiting. The platform is not a physical site, but symbolic transition space, located between the past and the present, the country and the city, tradition and modernity, where time is dominated by waiting.

In one of the penultimate scenes in the film, the troupe finally arrives at the bank of the Yellow River. It is here at the cradle of Chinese civilisation and the mythic 'homeland' of all China where the protagonists' journey finally nears its end. As Zhang Jun stands on the shore gazing out at the water, a freight barge slowly creeps into frame.

The barge is transporting a new shipment of colour televisions, the newest form of popular entertainment to infiltrate China's small towns in the late 1980s. The arrival of this mode of newly affordable 'home entertainment' marks a drastic shift away from the 'mass entertainment' of the past – the implication, of course, is also the dissolution of travelling entertainment troupes which will be rendered increasingly superfluous. This is the end of the Shenzhen Allstars Rock and Breakdance Electronic Band. The significance of this scene can also be seen from the fact that it was actually the very first scene that Jia and his crew shot, back in October 1999.[66] The beginning and the end, both tied to the flow of the Yellow River, the eternal mother beckoning her children home. Indeed, a few scenes later, Zhang Jun, Cui Mingliang and the remnants of the troupe return to Fenyang for the final time. As they prepare to return, the ever-fashionable Zhang Jun who by now has grown long hair in the

Zhang Jun lighting a cigarette as he gazes out over the Yellow River and sees a barge transporting colour television sets style of popular Chinese rock bands like Black Panther (Hei Bao), cuts his hair in a gesture that echoes Xiao Shan's haircut at the conclusion of *Xiao Shan Going Home*. Seeing a similarity with the rite young men and women undergo as they forsake the world for a monastic life, Xiaoping Lin has interpreted these hair-cutting sequences as 'resonant of an almost Buddhist ritual that renounces a male protagonist's shaky faith in Western values'.[67] The Chinese term for the ritual of entering a Buddhist monastery is *chu jia*, or literally 'leave home' – but here it is only on the eve of a return to the hometown that a similar rite is enacted. Ultimately, the troupe's travelling serves as the ultimate metaphor for China in transition. By the same token, the eventual end to their travels (and the beginning of domesticity) at the film's conclusion in 1989 also marks the (temporary) end of China's remarkable rise (and the beginning of a political clamp down), as marked by the Tiananmen Square massacre.

Back in Fenyang, Cui Mingliang's family is in shambles. His father has moved in with his mistress and never returns home. The father's new home beside a highway, a symbolic site that links the urban to the rural, also doubles as a store, indicating not only a breakdown between commercial and private spaces, but hinting at the lightning-fast pace at which even the 'sleepy city' of Fenyang is transforming. As Cui and his mother sit at home watching the popular television mini-series *Desires* (*Zhiwang*), the dialogue speaks of marriage, but Cui suddenly breaks the silence. 'Mom, why don't you just divorce him?' Here we have yet another inversion of an earlier scene where Cui's rejection by Yin Ruijuan was juxtaposed with his father's affair. Now, several years later it is Cui prodding his parents to divorce . . . just as he himself is about to be reunited with Yin Ruijuan.

While Cui Mingliang traversed China with the troupe, singing rock 'n' roll, breakdancing and carrying on a short-lived relationship with Li Xiaojuan, Yin Ruijuan remained back home in Fenyang. And as the country moved towards privatisation and various forms of entrepreneurial enterprises, Yin took a conservative

government job at the local tax bureau. During their long separation, several scenes indicated a mutual longing, such as Cui's silent telephone calls to his former love and Yin's melancholic dance, which hinted at nostalgia for her days as a dancer with the troupe. In the end the 'unlikely couple' are together back in Fenyang. During the final scene, Yin Ruijuan holds their infant child in her arms as a kettle of hot water is heating up on the stove. Cui Mingliang is slumped over crooked on the couch; having dozed off with a cigarette still in his hand.

In the background one can hear the television; the television that Cui Mingliang and Yin Ruijuan once crowded around in excitement now only provides additional background noise to lull the protagonist to sleep. Xiaoping Lin has identified the music playing as 'Travelling in Suzhou' ('Gusu xing'), a traditional song in sharp contrast to the modern rock 'n' roll of Zhang Xing's 'Platform'. But the chosen tune is also ironic in that this song of travel has now become the soundtrack for stagnation and the quotidian. Outside the front door one can clearly see the bastions of the city wall protruding against the horizon. The wall that once kept them apart has now sealed them in, the time for miracles has past. As Jia Zhangke describes, 'They were once rebellious, they once pursued their ideals

Return to the everyday: Cui Mingliang taking an afternoon nap and Yin Ruijuan holding their child as the kettle whistles and dreams, but in the end they return to everyday life – which is where most young people eventually end up. They return to the trappings of the everyday.'[68] And then, breaking the silence of this quiet afternoon comes the sound of the kettle whistling. Fade to black and the whistle continues. Suddenly it becomes apparent that this is the same whistle that opened the film just before the performance of *Train to Shaoshan*. It is in that moment that the sound of the whistling steam emerging from the teapot collapses into the sound of the train whistle which announced the beginning of the film. We are brought full circle as the train finally pulls into its station. The ridiculous whistle sound that the old troupe leader Xu once criticised Cui Mingliang for making has finally been perfected by the most everyday of household items and the elusive train that the protagonists had waited for on the platform is revealed to have been home all along.

4 *Unknown Pleasures*

In 2001, Jia Zhangke accepted a commission from the Jeonju Film Festival in Korea to shoot a digital short as part of a trilogy, the other two directors involved being John Akomfrah and Tsai Ming-liang. Jia chose Datong as the setting for his thirty-minute film, *In Public* (*Gonggong changsuo*), which documented a series of public spaces in and around the industrial city. It was the experience of shooting in Datong in the exciting new medium of digital that inspired Jia Zhangke to make *Unknown Pleasures* just two months after *In Public*. Just as *Xiao Wu* was largely inspired by the dynamic social and spatial environment of Fenyang in 1997, so too were *In Public* and *Unknown Pleasures* also inspired by another city in Jia's home province of Shanxi, Datong, and the remarkable changes taking place there. Jia spoke about what it was that initially drew him to the city:

> For me, Datong is a traditional city. Everyone in Shanxi always says how chaotic it is, describing the city as if it is some terrible place; but I wanted to go there for myself and have a look. At the time there was actually a rumour floating around that was quite enticing for me. People were saying that Datong was going to be relocated because the coalmines had already been exhausted of their resources, forcing the miners out of work. It was also the same time that everyone was talking about the development of western China, saying that all the miners would be sent to Xinjiang to extract petroleum. Because of this, it was rumoured that everyone was taking advantage of the opportunity to live it up.[69]

Whereas *Xiao Wu* ended with the shops along the main street of Fenyang being prepared for demolition, with *Unknown Pleasures* we enter the narrative via an environment of utter devastation and ruins. The industrial economy of Datong versus the primarily agricultural economy of Fenyang presented Jia with an opportunity to trace how industrial cities like Datong, which for decades had relied on state-sponsored factories for economic stability, have fared in the post-planned economy era. The keen attention to spaces and places prominently displayed throughout *In Public* can also be seen in the aesthetic vision of *Unknown Pleasures*. Throughout the film, the physical landscape of destruction again works as a powerful metaphor for the emotional, cultural and moral desolation of the characters as they blindly drift through towards an unknown destination.

Highlighting the plight of a group of teenagers and twenty-something outcasts in Datong, the juxtaposition with *Xiao Wu*, which took place just five years earlier, is quite startling. The dramatic social change revealed is further highlighted by shifting the narrative focus away from Wang Hongwei, the protagonist of *Xiao Wu* and *Platform* (who appears in *Unknown Pleasures* in a cameo), to a younger generation of social misfits who come of age in the post-Mao, post-socialist years. The moral predicament these characters find themselves in as they struggle to search for direction becomes a central theme as values and relationships remain in a state of constant flux. Jia's cinematic visions of destruction of demolition, which are evident throughout his earlier films, reach a disturbing climax in *Unknown Pleasures* as old buildings are torn down to make way for new architectural wonders that have yet to appear.

Unknown Pleasures was Jia's first narrative feature film shot entirely in digital. While Jia's trademark visual style remained, the shift to digital certainly brought a new texture and energy to his work. Director of photography Nelson Yu Lik Wai also commented on how the transition to digital affected the shoot:

[Shooting in digital] allowed us to be very flexible and relaxed, even changing some of our working methods. These included Jia Zhangke using a camera monitor for the very first time, and, as far as lighting went, our needs were

quite modest so in the end we shot the film with only a three-person camera crew and one lighting person. This helped us greatly save on both equipment and crew expenses. And because we were shooting onto digital tape, we didn't need to worry about the [film] cost. So there are quite a few shots where we could experiment with multiple angles and takes.[70]

The freedom digital film-making brought to the crew had an immediate effect on the visual style of *Unknown Pleasures*. The film marks a clear return to the bolder hand-held camerawork seen in *Xiao Wu*, while preserving many of the long shots that were so prevalent in *Platform*. From the opening tracking shot of Binbin (Zhao Weiwei) on a motorcycle traversing the streets of Datong, Jia seemed to be etching out a new aesthetic, which would be further developed as the film unfolds. At the same time, the turn to digital also had a fundamental impact on Jia and his crew's overall film-making approach. The entire film, from primary shooting to post-production, took less than three months, with much of the post-production including the final transfer from digital tape to celluloid carried out in France. Shooting in digital also brought a much higher degree of spontaneity and improvisation to the film, the screenplay of which was largely written (and continually revised)

Qiaoqiao strolling through one of *Unknown Pleasures*' many vistas of desolation during the shoot. While such an approach brings a newfound energy and edginess to the film, it at times seems also to lack the subtlety and layered nuance of Jia's earlier features.

Unknown Pleasures traces the lives of two best friends, Binbin and Xiao Ji (Wu Qiong), as they wander the streets of Datong in search of whatever adventures might await them. What motivates the pair is not the fevered idealism that once gripped Cui Mingliang and Zhang Jun in *Platform*, but a numb blindness and desperation. Children of the 1980s, Binbin and Xiao Ji represent the first genuine post-Mao generation, born and raised during Deng's Open Door era with no first-hand memories of China's communist past. No longer in school, unemployed and living at home with their single parents, Binbin and Xiao Ji traverse the city markets, clubs, billiard halls, karaoke parlours and other public spaces consuming the latest mainstream Chinese and western pop songs and movies that provide an alternative outlet to the glum world they see around them. Jin Liu has observed how Xiao Ji and Binbin 'never speak their parents' Datong Mandarin, implying that they are uncomfortable with their local identity, if not eager to abandon their roots altogether'.[71] Liu's observation alerts us to the fact that, even on the linguistic level, there already exists a fundamental disconnect between these drifting teenagers and their hometown, a detail that will make their ultimate predicament all the more desperate and tragic.

The traditionalist of the two, Binbin has a steady girlfriend in Yuanyuan (Zhou Qingfeng), a high school student applying to colleges. Xiao Ji, on the other hand, courts Qiaoqiao (Zhao Tao), a pretty dancer involved with a local thug. As their relationships deteriorate and what small dreams they carry die, Xiao Ji and Binbin plan a half-baked bank heist. Inspired by Quentin Tarantino's *Pulp Fiction* (1994) and a crop of Hong Kong action films, the friends' plot proves to be a futile attempt to use popular culture to transcend the hopeless reality around them – in the end, all it does is make their tragic reality more brutal.

The colour of money

One key to unlocking the tragedy behind Binbin and Xiao Ji's story is the central positioning of money and material gains throughout the film. Popular writer Liang Xiaosheng once described the uncontrollable thirst for money in contemporary China as a madness that was comparable only to the political fever of the Great Leap Forward and the Cultural Revolution.[72] Throughout the film we witness this infiltration of corruption and greed into the remnants of state enterprises as Qiao San (Li Zhubin), an official from the mining bureau, uses his connections to become a thug while the factory head rents out rooms to a 'hair salon', which serves as a thinly veiled cover for a prostitution house. But this 'money madness' truly emerges front and centre through Jia's narrative account of Xiao Ji and Binbin's adventure. The material messages that inundate the characters' lives not only become a central theme of the film, but the primary mechanism that transforms what could have been a typical coming-of-age story into a tragic-comic parable of undoing.

In *Xiao Wu* money is also an important theme, but it is never as centrally figured as in *Unknown Pleasures*. It may seem curious that money should become more of a central fixation for a group of nineteen-year-old kids than for a pickpocket purportedly consumed with nothing but stealing. The rift, however, lies in the simple fact that stealing is only a means to an end for Xiao Wu. His actions are dictated not so much by money, but by his relationships; hence the steep increase in thefts just before Jin Xiaoyong's marriage (so he can present a respectable gift) or when courting Hu Meimei (so he can shower her with small gifts). For Binbin and Xiao Ji, the pursuit of money has become the end in itself, their desire a product of a pervasive commercial culture and pop-culture gangster fantasies. Xiao Wu was a thief with a conscious, desperately holding on to his own moral codes and notions of 'brotherhood' and 'righteousness' even amid a whirlwind of change; Cui Mingliang had passion, ideals and once strived to transform his fate, but Binbin and Xiao Ji seem to lack these traits, often appearing petty, jealous and selfish as they blindly pursue their own 'unknown pleasures'.

In one of the very first scenes of the film, taking place in a converted bus station waiting room, Binbin and Xiao Ji are sitting on a bench when Xiao Wu (Wang Hongwei), now sporting a short crew-cut and sunglasses, struts in to tell them about a new job opportunity with Mongolian King Liquor. The scene is the first glimpse of the protagonists' desperation to find work, especially Binbin, who is recently laid off. When Xiao Wu demands a 10 yuan 'introduction fee', pay-off for the information, it is already clear that this is no longer a world revolving around *guanxi* or 'relationships and favours' (which were symbolically destroyed in *Xiao Wu*), but a world that revolves around naked monetary exchange. The ambient sounds of television and radio broadcasts, which Jia Zhangke used to such great effect in his earlier films, here echo the materialist message. The scene ends with an announcement about an upcoming lottery while a group of laid-off workers gamble outside. With increasing unemployment and desperation setting in, new 'cures' for society's ills have been introduced, booze to provide escape from the pain and gambling to provide false hope for the dreamers. The scene concludes with Xiao Wu being cuffed and dragged off by a pair of undercover policemen, surely the pickpocket of old has not changed his ways – but society clearly has. Unlike the tragic power of his arrest at the climax of *Xiao Wu*, here Xiao Wu's arrest is but a curious, almost humorous, sidenote. Nor does Xiao Wu's arrest attract the gawking crowds it once did; in *Unknown Pleasure*'s world of crooks and swindlers such scenes are only another scene in people's quotidian reality.

The discourse of economic change continues to inundate the cinematic narrative as the film progresses, punctuating the twists and turns in the characters' lives. For Binbin and Yuanyuan, their relationship plays out in a seedy karaoke club where patrons watch porn videos or use the room for illicit rendezvous with prostitutes or lovers. But there in that dark environment where moans break out from neighbouring rooms, Binbin and Yuanyuan struggle to overcome their timidity and develop their relationship. There they sing along to saccharine pop hits from Taiwan and watch movies. During one of their dates at the karaoke club, Binbin and Yuanyuan sit side-by-side in a private room watching *Uproar in Heaven* (*Danao tiangong*) (1964), a classic animated version of *Journey to the West* (*Xiyou ji*), when the topic of China's entry into the WTO comes up. Binbin, taking the indifferent rebellious attitude of the Monkey King, comments, 'WTO is just another money thing.' By the end of the film we learn that Yuanyuan is leaving him to pursue a degree in international trade. Here the very *local* and *direct* effects of the WTO and the increasing drive towards globalisation is felt quite palpably. Eventually, even Binbin himself will brag about his own 'imaginary job' in international trade (just as stock market updates are announced in the background). At other times, the place of money in the film's narrative is highlighted not through its looming power, but through its notable absence. A colleague of Binbin's mother comes calling to announce a factory meeting that she must attend, meanwhile the factory hasn't paid its workers in months. The shell of the communist bureaucracy remains, but the commitment to provide for its people has been shattered by the new capitalist reality. In the absence of money, Binbin's mother instead turns to Fulun Gong, another means of filling the void left by the collapse of communist ideology and the transcendent revolutionary fervour of Mao's China. (The effects of this new cult religious group are displayed in a later scene when Xiao Ji watches television coverage of Fulun Gong followers committing self-immolation in Tiananmen Square.)

It is not only the conception of materialism that dominates the film's narrative, but also the actual *image* of money that becomes a key visual trope that is repeatedly returned to. The influence of Mao gradually retreated into the background during the historical transition of *Platform*, emerging as a trinket of nostalgia to hang on the rear-view mirror in *Xiao Wu*. But with no new ideology to replace Maoism besides 'to get rich is glorious', money eventually

emerges as the new state ideology. Even the old adage coined to
describe the hope of the future promised by the Four Modernisations,
'look towards the future' (*xiang qian kan*) has become replaced with
the homophonic saying 'look towards money' (*xiang qian kan*), a
telling revision that captures the displacement of the future as it is sold
out for the bottom line. This sell-out is paraded throughout *Unknown
Pleasures* as the gangster Qiao San sticks a 100 yuan note to his head
to tip a nightclub singer – a scene that Xiao Ji and Binbin observe up
close and which no doubt inspires their own materialist dreams.
When a single US dollar is passed around between everyone in Xiao
Ji's family apartment it becomes the source of endless speculation and
wonder. The dialogue accompanying this second example captures
their utter fascination with this symbol of prosperity:

XIAO JI'S FATHER: What's this weird money?

CUSTOMER: Boss, you're rich! That's a US dollar!

XIAO JI: A dollar? A damn US dollar!

XIAO JI'S FATHER: Can I use it?

CUSTOMER: Why not? Change it at the bank.

XIAO JI: Binbin, my old man hit the jackpot!

BINBIN: What's this worth?

CUSTOMER: I'd say easily more than 1,000 yuan.

BINBIN: 1,000 yuan!

CUSTOMER: At least.

XIAO JI: I'm rich boys!

Qiao San tipping a singer with a 100 yuan note as Qiaoqiao looks on; Xiao Ji's father
scrutinising a US dollar bill

The almost comic overestimation of the dollar's value (which is actually worth approximately 8 yuan) speaks not only to their misunderstanding of its actual worth, but also to their misunderstanding of the cumulative impact the state economic reforms are having on their actual lives. Note the stark contrast between the dollar as the ultimate image of prosperity versus the small dilapidated single-room shack father and son share. The emphasis Jia places on the materiality of the dollar and fetishisation of this near-holy object can be seen as it is passed around the various characters, exchanging hands no less than nine times over the course of the short scene. In this emphasis on the object is an implicit irony of everyday people's ignorance of the very object they desire and strive so hard to achieve. As the dollar repeatedly trades hands, the scene also conjures memories of a similar moment in *Xiao Wu*, when the Liang family passes around Xiao Wu's new beeper, curiously examining this new high-tech gadget. But here a fascination with technology is replaced with a much more base fascination with hard currency as everything is reduced to a more base level.

Intricately tied to the increasing money fever that sweeps the narrative is the special attention devoted to international relations, globalism and especially the USA. Often the place of these interrelated themes functions as a means to further emphasise the desperation and material lack of the protagonists. As an announcement of the decision to allow Beijing to host the 2008 Summer Olympics plays to an excited crowd sitting outside around a small television set, Xiao Ji looks anything but elated having just been beaten by Qiao San's thugs. With this scene lies yet another example of Jia's juxtaposition of history with the everyday (like the Hong Kong handover in *Xiao Wu* or the Tiananmen incident in *Platform*). In this case, however, such grand events seem to leave the protagonists feeling even more frustrated and dejected. The next shot is of the grey soviet-style apartment building surrounded by polluted skies and dirt – clearly, the Olympic news has little impact on the lives of Xiao Ji, Qiaoqiao and everyone else in Datong. In another such scene, news of the US spy plane that landed in Chinese territory in 2001 appears on television, just minutes before a loud explosion rocks the town. A startled Xiao Ji leaps out of his chair and approaches the front door, 'Shit! Are the Americans attacking?' This anti-American rhetoric and latent fears of a US attack are juxtaposed with the everyday detail of Binbin drinking a can of Coca-Cola. As fears of American imperialist aggression pervade the media, 'soft' forms of American cultural and economic infiltration are already silently at play as evidenced by the Coca-Cola Binbin is drinking.[73] (Jia had previously highlighted a crushed can of Coke towards the end of *Xiao Wu*, where it appeared before Xiao Wu and his sister as a piece of capitalist garbage impeding their way.)

The bomb explosion that Binbin hears also foreshadows the destruction of his own newfound dreams to join the army. Binbin's decision to apply for the military has very little to do with any projected American imperialist threat; it is instead inspired by much more pragmatic factors. With his mother not receiving paycheques and himself unemployed, joining the military is simply the last resort (and a convenient way to leave Datong for Beijing where Yuanyuan will be going to school). Xiao Ji arrives at the hospital the next morning for his mandatory blood test to join the army, but he will soon be struck down by a very different assault – a test result stating he has contracted hepatitis. The disease will not only disqualify him for military service, but the doctor's orders that he not kiss for fear of spreading this highly contagious disease will also doom his relationship with Yuanyuan.

From international economy to the economy of relationships, Jia Zhangke artfully demonstrates the impact of new global flows and material desires on interpersonal relationships. In a scene at the hospital, Xiao Ji and Binbin run into Qiaoqiao who is there to look after her sick father. In a rush to pay the required 2,000 yuan in hospital fees, Qiaoqiao gives Xiao Ji her bankbook and password and asks him to withdraw the money for her. While at the bank withdrawing the money, Xiao Ji sees his own father, who is (unsuccessfully) attempting to exchange his single US dollar.

The synchronicity at play when Xiao Ji and Qiaoqiao are linked through their fathers introduces an irony that will not be fully revealed until one of the final scenes in the film. Xiao Ji helps furnish the money that will save Qiaoqiao's father, but later it will be Xiao Ji's father that supplies the money to buy Qiaoqiao. The cycle of exchange is completed when we consider the origin of that single magical US dollar, which can be traced to a promotional lottery launched by Mongolian King Liquor, the very product that Qiaoqiao dances to sell.

One of the few moments of the film in which Qiaoqiao seems to escape from the web of commodification and consumption that entraps her is when she first removes the China-girl wig she has worn for virtually the entire film. For the first time, Qiaoqiao seems to evade the control of Qiao San and begins to articulate her own desires, as evidenced by quickly developing her relationship with Xiao Ji. It is only *after* removing her wig that the butterfly motif (present on her shirts and costumes throughout the film) is fully revealed. The butterfly first emerges as she and Xiao Ji find themselves in a hotel room where Qiaoqiao draws a large butterfly on the hotel mirror. A few shots later, the camera captures the butterfly tattoo on her shoulder. The motif is further embellished when she explains the famous fable about Zhuangzi's butterfly to Xiao Ji, which she boils down to the simplified maxim, 'Do whatever makes you feel good.'

The story, is one of the most beloved in classical Chinese Daoist philosophy:

Once Zhuang Zhou dreamt he was a butterfly, a butterfly flitting and fluttering around, happy with himself and doing as he pleased. He didn't know he was Zhuang Zhou. Suddenly he woke up and there he was, solid and unmistakable Zhuang Zhou. But he didn't know if he was a Zhuang Zhou

who had dreamt he was a butterfly, or a butterfly dreaming he was Zhuang Zhou. Between Zhuang Zhou and a butterfly there must be *some* distinction! This is called the Transformation of Things.[74]

The parable here represents Qiaoqiao's own self-conscious narrative of identity as she struggles with her own difficult choices between her unrealistic dreams and the cruelty of reality. The conundrum she faces is to fulfil her own desires or those of Qiao San. The wig represents her cocoon, it is the costume that Qiao San and others desire, and it is only in those fleeting moments together with Xiao Ji that she seems to regain a bit of herself. In this sense, those fleeting scenes in the hotel room are reminiscent of Xiao Wu naked in the bathhouse, both ephemeral moments in which the protagonists are stripped bare of all the physical and symbolic restrictions that weigh them down and allowed to soar. But, as was the case of Xiao Wu's fleeting happiness, so too the life of a butterfly is short indeed. After a few scenes stripped down as herself with Xiao Ji, she reappears with an even denser disguise, wearing a bright blue wig to receive her new client – Xiao Ji's father. Meanwhile, the butterfly she drew has now been transferred to Xiao Ji, who wears it on his shirt, allowing it to freely carry him off towards certain destruction.[75]

Butterfly dreams: Qiaoqiao drawing a butterfly in *Unknown Pleasures*

Pop culture and postmodern pastiche

From the story about Zhuang Zhou and the butterfly, Qiaoqiao goes on to reference another story from the Zhuangzi, the opening chapter 'Free and Easy Wandering' ('Xiaoyao you'). Qiaoqiao's explanation of its meaning, 'Do whatever makes you feel good', further emphasises the whims of the butterfly, 'flitting and fluttering around, happy with himself and doing as he pleased'. The irony, of course, is that this dream-like parable of freedom, wandering and an easy life has been told to Qiaoqiao by Qiao San, the very person controlling her fate and, in this case, even her fantasies. Tonglin Lu has also observed that 'the tattooed butterfly on Qiaoqiao's chest reveals her sexual dependency, because it reminds her of Qiao San, the first owner of her body'.[76] In this context, the story and its origin double the objectified US dollar that appears before her at the end of the film, a bill that represents freedom and dreams, but actually also originates with the same commercial liquor troupe that objectifies and exploits her. The Chinese title of 'Free and Easy Wandering', 'Xiaoyao you', shares two characters with the original title of the film *Ren xiaoyao*, which brings us to the other referent in the film's title.

Like *Platform*, *Unknown Pleasures* also takes its name from the title of a song – actually, *two* pop songs. Ping Ri has observed the varying meanings 'Unknown Pleasures' carries for different characters; for Qiaoqiao and Qiao San the referent is Zhuangzi's philosophy of, in the words of Qiaoqiao, 'Do whatever makes you feel good', but for Binbin, his dose of 'Unknown Pleasures' comes via the Chinese pop song 'Ren xiaoyao', by Richie Jen, a popular Taiwan crooner.[77] The song is used numerous times in the film, often during crucial moments in the development of the story. The international title, *Unknown Pleasures*, is inspired by a few lines from one of the director's notebooks about an 'indescribable exhilaration'; when cinematographer Nelson Yu Lik Wai saw those words, he immediately thought of the 1979 album *Unknown Pleasures* by the British rock band Joy Division. (Yu had previously named his own feature *Love Will Tear Us Apart* [*Tianshang renjian*] after a song by this group.) This layered title points to the dual pop-culture referents, further reinforcing the unique form of cultural hybridity *Unknown Pleasures* represents and attempts to negotiate as it situates itself at the crossroads of east and west, the Chinese and the foreign, the local and global. This hybridity is, of course, further conflated by the classical allusion to Zhuangzi and Daoist philosophy hidden beneath.

Richie Jen's version of 'Ren xiaoyao' is first played during the open auditions for the Mongolian King Liquor Troupe, which also doubles as a public performance. The lyrics ring out in the background as Qiaoqiao ventures into the crowd shaking hands with the audience members.

> Whatever sorrows come
> Whatever regrets come
> As long as there's someone who
> Understands my love
> Whatever suffering comes
> Whatever weariness comes
> I follow the wind
> I roam happy and carefree
> A hero unashamed of his humble origins
> Many are my ambitions
> Proud is my heart
> Only the word love
> Lingers in my mind
> All my life
> I've pursued it in vain.

Significant is the fact that this scene also marks the very first time that Xiao Ji sees Qiaoqiao – and makes physical contact with the star dancer when she shakes his hand. The song recurs a second time many scenes later when Yuanyuan and Binbin are in the karaoke club on one of their dates. The scene begins with an extreme close-up of the karaoke monitor, which is displaying Ritchie Jen's music video for

the song. As the video progresses, the camera pans to the young couple sitting on the couch. By the second refrain, Binbin and Yuanyuan begin to gently sing along with the bubblegum pop song. It is only towards the end of the song that their hands embrace as they softly sway back and forth.

It is certainly no coincidence that the first physical contact between the two young couples plays out with 'Ren xiaoyao' as the background soundtrack. The lyrics, which speak of a carefree hero living a life of sorrow and unrequited love, hints at both a bloated sense of imaginary heroism and the fact that neither love story will have a very optimistic outcome. It is also in the scene at the karaoke club that Yuanyuan first expresses her wish to study international trade in Beijing – her own carefree desire. After initially uniting the lovers, the song appears again during the brutal climax when Binbin, arrested for a botched robbery plot, sings the song unaccompanied in the police station as the screen abruptly cuts to black.

Through these three appropriations of the song we witness not just the evolution of the story, but also the transformation of song itself, as it is repeatedly remade. During the first scene in which the song is used, it helps create a festive and upbeat atmosphere. The original song blasts from the speakers, with an added rhythm track to accentuate its beat, as Richie Jen's voice rings out to a crowd of ecstatic audience members and a troupe of vibrant dancers. When the song recurs in the karaoke room, as Binbin and Yuanyuan stare at the monitor and quietly listen in that dimly lit room, it is clear that the mood has significantly changed. By the time the young

First contacts: Xiao Ji and Qiaoqiao shaking hands and Binbin and Yuanyuan interlocking hands, both to the tune of 'Ren xiaoyao' or 'Unknown Pleasures' couple begin to quietly murmur the lyrics along with the singer, the song suddenly takes on a distinctly melancholic feeling. This melancholy is taken to a new level in the final scene when Binbin revisits the song via an a cappella version – forced by the police officer watching over him. Even the volume of the song undergoes a constriction as it goes from being broadcast at a public event with amplified speakers to a small television set until it ultimately comes to us through a sole, weak human voice. Along the way, the saccharine song transforms from a pure pop product into a highly personal statement about the characters' predicament, ultimately challenging the ideal of heroic masculinity espoused by the original song. At the same time, the most ironic transformation of 'Ren xiaoyao' occurs as it goes from a tool to market a product and entertain Binbin (and the rest of the audience) to a heart-breaking cry Binbin releases to entertain a bored police officer. As in *Xiao Wu* and *Platform*, Jia Zhangke again demonstrates the sublime power of popular music to transcend and transform.

The other pop-culture text that the characters imitate to equally disastrous effect is Quentin Tarantino's *Pulp Fiction*. Xiao Ji excitedly describes the film's diner robbery scene to Qiaoqiao, his excitement building until the scene makes a rapid cut to a disco where they are seen imitating the iconic dance between Uma Thurman and John Travolta (with this scene, an alternate inspiration behind Qiaoqiao's China-girl wig also suddenly becomes apparent). A similar romanticised reinterpretation of what is seen on television also occurs earlier when Xiao Ji sees a TV news interrogation of a prisoner, a report meant as a lesson to the public to discourage crime (a broadcast that may just as well be of Xiao Wu's arrest) that instead inspires excitement in Xiao Ji. In the end, it is this same set of *Pulp Fiction* fantasies that drives Xiao Ji and Binbin to strap fake explosives to their bodies in a bank heist that ultimately proves as pathetic as it is tragic. McGrath has described the scene as 'one of the most morose and anticlimactic bank heist scenes in cinema history'[78] – even the film itself cannot resist its own internal commentary on

how neither of the would-be-robbers even look the part. As the duo approaches the China Construction Bank to pull off their ill-conceived caper, we realise that it is their own future that has been stolen by a dark world of desperation, exploitation and unrealistic dreams.

In the aftermath of the robbery Xiao Ji escapes on his motorcycle, leaving Binbin to take the fall. As Binbin is left alone in the police station, guarded by a single officer watching the television, we are immediately brought back to a very similar scene that takes place during the final moments of *Xiao Wu*. Here we see a distinct shift from Jia's engagement with pop-culture texts (songs, television programmes, movies) to a self-reflexive engagement with *his own* previous films.

This engagement is revealed through a synthesis and extension of the forms, ideas and themes of *Xiao Wu* and *Platform* (which will be discussed further in the following section), as well as a series of bolder and more humorous references to his earlier films. These references are immediately evident in the early scenes of *Unknown Pleasures* through a series of cameos by Wang Hongwei and none other than Jia Zhangke himself. Although Jia had played minor roles in his early student film *Xiao Shan Going Home* and *Xiao Wu*, here he takes on the recurring role of Mr Ma, a mentally handicapped man who stands in various public places singing opera in his undershirt. The film also reintroduces Wang Hongwei who revisits the character of Xiao Wu as a parody of himself. Such scenes bring a tone of surreal camp to *Unknown Pleasures*, a quality largely

The policeman and the thief: Xiao Wu and the policeman at the station in *Xiao Wu* and a similar scene with Binbin and a policeman in *Unknown Pleasures* absent from the earlier films in the trilogy. Although Jia had flirted with tongue-in-cheek humour in his earlier films (such as announcing Yu Lik Wai's name as a wanted man during the post-Tiananmen crackdown), here he ups the ante with a more pronounced breed of self-parody. This is made most evident in one of the final scenes when Binbin is hawking bootleg DVDs on the street when Xiao Wu approaches to ask if he has copies of *Xiao Wu*, *Platform*, or Yu Lik Wai's feature *Love Will Tear Us Apart*. As film-maker and critic Kevin Lee has observed, 'Jia can't even locate himself in the world of his own films, ruefully regarding the inability of his work to connect back to its source of inspiration.'[79]

The pastiche of different textual referents, including numerous engagements with the previous films in the trilogy, coupled with the widespread infiltration of global capitalism, make *Unknown Pleasures* a much more postmodern film than Jia's earlier work. The texture of the film as a digital pastiche of intertextual references and narrative responses to earlier themes in the trilogy is further enhanced by the chosen medium. Jia's playful engagement with the world of simulacra and reproduction is highlighted in the aforementioned scene featuring Xiao Wu trying to purchase bootleg DVDs. This marks a new world of cheap, plastic replicas rising from the ashes of the demolished city. At the same time, we are led to question the authenticity of not only the product, but even the buyer. Is that really Xiao Wu, the pickpocket of Fenyang? Or just another cheap imitation? Has the 'artisan pickpocket' whose pathos and

Jia Zhangke as Mr Ma, the mentally challenged streetside opera singer and the return of Xiao Wu, looking to buy bootleg Jia Zhangke and Yu Lik Wai DVDs from Binbin

plight once so moved audiences been reduced to a mere self-parody? While the continuity of characters between different Jia Zhangke films is intentionally challenged and blurred, the extension of his cinematic universe through similar themes is quite strong. And the cheap copies (of both DVDs and Xiao Wu) paraded at the end of *Unknown Pleasures* can certainly be read as a prelude to the plastic universe of simulacra Jia would later construct for *The World*.

Going nowhere

The on-the-road sequence that begins *Unknown Pleasures* also continues a similar motif that began Jia's two previous features. *Platform* opens with an imaginary train (performed on stage) before the troupe board a dark bus as the credits roll; in *Xiao Wu* the very first scene shows the protagonist boarding a bus, but here the opening shot features a frontal tracking shot of Binbin on his motorcycle racing through the crowded streets of Datong. The shot is immediately reminiscent of the sequences in *Platform* depicting the troupe entering and leaving the city. However, unlike that earlier film, which only sparingly used such shots to emphasise the restless movement and longing for the outside world of the protagonists, here a very different aesthetic of movement is announced from the outset. Unlike the rich expressions of the troupe singing goodbye to their friends and Cui Mingliang crying in sadness as they leave the city for the first time, the look on Binbin's face as he traverses the streets on his borrowed motorcycle is one of blank numbness. Tonglin Lu has also pointed out the 'sense of entrapment' implicit in this and other motorcycle tracking shots in *Unknown Pleasures*. 'Although the frame is changing, the tracking shot creates the illusion that the protagonist is trapped in the same position and in the same location, despite his spatial displacement. Regardless of how fast Binbin moves, he can never break away from the frame imposed on him.'[80] As the final instalment of Jia's 'Hometown Trilogy' opens, any sign of the excitement that marked the earlier voyage has been erased.

Whereas even *seeing* a train was a novelty for the protagonists in *Platform*, the continued economic transformation China has undergone in the ensuing years has brought motorcycles within the grasp of the boys in *Unknown Pleasures* – a luxury that would have been unimaginable for Cui Mingliang or Xiao Wu. However, as Binbin and Xiao Ji traverse the city on their motorcycle, there seems to be no true destination in sight. Instead, they blindly meander through the dilapidated cityscape of Datong, often following a series of local performances that promote 'Mongolian King Liquor', where they can get free drinks and gawk at the young dancers.

This is also where Jia Zhangke makes what is perhaps his most powerful intertextual intervention, again not in reference to pop music, *Pulp Fiction*, or Ah Q, but to his previous film, *Platform*. In *Platform* we witnessed the transformation of the song and dance troupe from a government-sponsored propaganda work unit to a privatised Allstars Rock and Breakdance Electronic Band. In its latter incarnation under Song Yongping's tutelage, the rock and breakdance band toured China with Shenzhen serving as the troupe's fictional hometown. In a highly self-referential move, Jia Zhangke reintroduces a similar song and dance troupe in *Unknown Pleasures*. But this time the troupe has gone through an additional phase of metamorphosis that further conflates the meaning of 'performing China'. The imaginary cosmopolitan hometown of Shenzhen – site of modernity and transnational flows – has been replaced with Mongolia, a site even more rural than Datong that conjures images of nomads and grasslands. Amid the cacophony of an industrial city in transition, the object of longing is no longer the cosmopolitan city, but an idyllic return to a simple life – a more traditional conception of the *guxiang*. But even more startling is not the implied topographical shift, but the symbolic transformation of the troupe itself. While Jia previously traced the transition of the troupe from a state-run propaganda unit to a privatised, self-sustaining business, here the Mongolian King Liquor Troupe has become completely consumed by the powers of commercialisation.

Whereas the Shenzhen Allstars Rock and Breakdance Electronic Band performed 'Platform' and an assortment of Chinese rock and pop hits that spoke to their generation's ideals and disillusionment, articulating a new breed of modern youthful rebellion, in *Unknown Pleasures* the troupe itself has been transformed into nothing more than a local travelling commercial. Also lost in this transformation is any notion of genuine musical performance, as the electric instruments of the rock and breakdance band are exchanged for prerecorded pop songs leaving only the spectacle of dance. Once a train of dreams, the politics of performance have been reduced to a vulgar advertisement for selling cheap alcohol – a product that perhaps replaces trains and buses as the only realistic means of 'escape'. In an age where the 'product' and the 'bottom line' rule the day, art and performance is no longer used to convey political ideals or even personal dreams, they simply become tools to serve corporate interests and fuel consumerist desires.

At the same time, the ideals and dreams of the previous generation have been shattered. Cui Mingliang once struggled against the burden of tradition to remake himself as an 'art worker', but in *Unknown Pleasures* art has devolved into simple commercial propaganda. With this devolution also comes an end to the curiosity to venture beyond the hometown to see what lies beyond. The longing for the 'dazzling world' of Shenzhen and Guangzhou that Zhang Jun spoke of has been displaced by more modest desires. The troupe never leaves the confines of Datong and, with only a few exceptions, the only mention of venturing beyond the confines of the

The 'Mongolian King' hosting a promotional event and Qiaoqiao on stage during another outdoor event to promote Mongolian King Liquor, while Xiao Ji and Binbin stand at the far right city come in the form of going to Hongdu to see she-males perform or Yunwang to see Russian prostitutes. In *Unknown Pleasures*, lofty dreams have been replaced by increasingly perverse forms of base local entertainment.

One of the few attempts to break through the confines of Datong comes through Binbin's attempt to join the military. But even here, such dreams are conveyed with much irony and scepticism. While, during the Mao years, being a soldier in the People's Liberation Army was the ultimate dream of countless children who fantasised about idealised soldiers like Huang Jiguang, Dong Cunrui and Lei Feng, Binbin expresses a real reluctance about joining. Here we are presented with the shifting status of the soldier in modern China, from a socialist hero that children fantasise about one day becoming to the new post-Tiananmen conception of a soldier as a last resort job for dead-end kids in provincial towns. Realising that he is without other options, Binbin finally goes to register only to discover that an undiscovered case of hepatitis disqualifies him from service, also effectively cutting off any opportunity to leave Datong for Beijing.

Unknown Pleasures both opens and closes with images of movement – providing a strong juxtaposition between the image of Binbin on the motorcycle going through the streets of Datong and Xiao Ji on the same motorcycle in the penultimate scene. But unlike *Platform*, the characters never go anywhere. In *Platform* the characters are on a journey, but in *Unknown Pleasures* they don't know where to go. At the end of the film comes the news that the Beijing–Datong Highway has finally been completed. But having had his chance to go Beijing to serve in the military taken away, Binbin won't be taking that road, especially after his arrest for bank robbery. And nor will Xiao Ji as his motorcycle runs out of gas in the middle of the street. The motorcycle's failure during this crucial moment surely speaks of a much greater cultural and spiritual failure. It is a hurdle visually foreshadowed much earlier when Xiao Ji couldn't get his motorcycle up a steep hill near the factory housing projects where he lives. Jia spoke about these scenes during an interview:

In the original screenplay there is nothing wrong with the motorcycle, so that scene was something that came out spontaneously during shooting. Suddenly the motorcycle wouldn't go up the hill and began to stall. I should have yelled cut right there but I discovered that the actor's expression at that moment was so close to what the character was going through. He looked so anxious, he wanted to make it up the hill, he wanted to get through his youth, and to get the scene right. He kept trying and I kept shooting. Only after this scene did I get the idea of revisiting the stalled-out motorcycle again at the end of the film. So in the penultimate scene we decided that we would have him run out of gas, but then it rained and the scene was brought to a whole other level.[81]

This series of mechanical failures can also be read as symbolic of Xiao Ji's internal failure of masculinity, as he repeatedly stumbles in his attempts to win over Qiaoqiao, the star dancer of the Mongolian King Liquor Troupe. But the ultimate failure, or breakdown, arrives when we see Xiao Ji's own father approach Qiaoqiao, offering 50 yuan for her services. She initially refuses, but he quickly offers her a single US dollar – the same dollar that had been such a focal part of the film's earlier narrative and that he had been unable to exchange at the bank – with Qiaoqiao's implied acceptance we bear witness to the ultimate betrayal. For Xiao Ji, this scene marks a dual deception by both his father and girlfriend, but for Qiaoqiao, this crucial moment represents the final stage in her own process of commodification.

Another key to the film's strategy of stagnation is revealed through extensive use of vehicles and locations traditionally associated with travel, which are all converted into immobile signposts that all movement has been suspended. Among these sites is the bus station waiting room converted into dance hall and a public bus converted into restaurant. Such spatial conversions of former public transportation hubs and vehicles into refurbished money-making vehicles for the new capitalist economy is not unique to Jia's film (Zhang Yimou's tragic comedy *Happy Times* [*Xingfu shiguang*]

[2000] also featured the conversion of an abandoned freight car into a love motel). Here, however, the abandoned vehicles and former transformation spaces become centre stage for much of the main action and a key component of the film's *mise en scène*. We should also not forget the importance of these spaces and vehicles in *In Public*, the documentary that inspired *Unknown Pleasures*, which also featured extensive use of bus station waiting rooms and public buses. And as Ping Ri has observed,[82] much of the key action between various characters transpires inside these broken vehicles – the first 'kiss' between Qiaoqiao and Xiao Ji takes place in the back of a van, the last fight between Qiao San and Qiaoqiao occurs in a converted bus and the final break-up between Yuanyuan and Binbin takes place in a converted bus station waiting room. And while all of these important sequences play out inside vehicles or spaces associated with movement, none of them are ever in motion. Although Yuanyuan and Binbin's break-up takes place in the converted waiting room, they are not waiting for anything – at least not Binbin, whose future has been cut off by a series of missed and stolen opportunities.

It is also in that final meeting between Binbin and Yuanyuan at the converted station waiting room that the site's latent meaning as a place of movement and change is tapped into. As the couple sits in a side booth, we realise that this is the first – and last – time they ever sit face-to-face. In the karaoke club they frequented, they would always sit side-by-side, facing the television screen, but here for the very first time they seem to face one another's reality. Binbin presents his sweetheart with a Motorola mobile phone as a final parting gift before she leaves for Beijing to study international trade. (The mobile phone will go on to become a central motif and metaphor for both materialism and globalisation in Jia's subsequent film *The World*.) It is only at that moment that Yuanyuan finally asks Binbin to kiss her – is this an expression of true love? A kiss goodbye? Or perhaps just a reciprocal gesture having accepted his expensive gift of a mobile phone? But in the end it is of no consequence, having tested positive for hepatitis, Binbin cannot even kiss his love; his only response a mute attempt at feigned ambivalence to cover up his pain.

As Yuanyuan rides off on her bicycle, an announcement comes over the loudspeaker, 'Attention all passengers for Taiyuan, the bus is now ready for boarding. Attention all passengers for Yuanping, Xinzhou, Taiyuan, please board now, immediate departure.' It is at that moment that Jia Zhangke draws a wry comparison to Cui Mingliang and Yin Ruijuan's break-up in *Platform*, which was also immediately followed by a loudspeaker announcement of a departing bus. In Cui's case, it foreshadowed his departure from home and the beginning of his adventure . . . but here the implication is far less romantic. In *Unknown Pleasures*, the hometown is the first and only stop in the protagonists' dead-end journey. Having given up his dreams of joining the army (which was already only a back-up plan) and lost his love, the only journey Binbin can make is to the local 'hair salon', where he curls up in the fetal position and seeks comfort from the older prostitute that had once unsuccessfully courted him. On that first occasion he left abruptly, not wanting to betray his love for Yuanyuan, but now there is nothing left to betray.

Binbin seeking consolation at the massage parlour

One of the key songs highlighted in *Platform* was the popular hit 'Young Friends Come Together' ('Nianqing pengyou lai xianghui') which spoke of the hope and excitement for a brighter future.

> In twenty years we will meet again
> During a time when the skies, the land,
> The nation will certainly be more beautiful.

In *Platform*, after the troupe leader Xu sings the song during an official performance, the troupe members rework the song with new lyrics that they sing from the back of the truck:

> In twenty years we will meet again,
> I'll have seven or eight wives
> And a whole stable of kids.

This comic reworking earns Zhang Jun and Cui Mingliang a lecture from Xu, who criticises them for belittling the one-child policy in favour of a feudal worldview that promotes polygamy and multiple children. The revisionist lyrics that seem to mock the promise of the future provide an ironic context for the song to play out. But the true irony comes with *Unknown Pleasures*, almost exactly twenty years after 'Young Friends Come Together' was initially released, in 1980. Two decades after the promise of a brighter future, Jia Zhangke makes good on the date but the reality is not terribly bright. Binbin and Xiao Ji live in a world where the skies are grey and the land is a virtual demolition site. For this new generation of 'young friends' their story does not end with them 'coming together', but rather betrayal as Xiao Ji abandons Binbin (a restaging of Xiaoyong's betrayal of Xiao Wu?) and the nation is caught in the throes of sweeping reforms that leave them both behind.

5 Coda: From Home to the World

Throughout Jia's corpus of works, though the hometown may be caught amid economic devastation, reconstruction and shifting moral alliances, it is always a place to come home to – the site of longing and nostalgia. Home is where Xiao Shan and countless migrant workers long to go back to for the New Year (*Xiao Shan Going Home, The World*); it is the site of return for the drama troupe and where Yin Ruijuan lies waiting (*Platform*); it is where Meimei telephones when she needs consolation from the bitter life she leads as a hostess girl; and even Xiao Wu returns to his family after his friendships and relationships fall apart (*Xiao Wu*). But as the characters in Jia Zhangke's films live in a world of constant destruction and transformation, so too the family proves increasingly susceptible to fracture and change, from Cui Mingliang's father's abandonment of his family for another woman (*Platform*), to Xiao Wu's exile by the father (*Xiao Wu*), to the broken family relationships in *Unknown Pleasures*, we witness not only destruction of the physical environment surrounding these characters, but the deterioration of the familial ties that keep them together. Born in the 1980s after the implementation of the one-child policy, the alienation and loneliness Binbin and Xiao Ji face is further enhanced by their respective single-parent families, another telling signpost of familial deterioration.

Fractured, broken, or compromised as the family may be, in Jia's early films it is at the very least always *there*, intimately tied to the hometown for which one yearns. This theme is taken to another level in *Still Life* where the physical place of return is not only destroyed, but submerged, shattering the emotional, physical and material coordinates of home. No longer can one even count on their family even being there. As the two protagonists of *Still Life* haunt the ruins of Fengjie searching for their lost family members, we realise Jia has taken his politics of destruction and yearning for home to the ultimate end. The choice of Fengjie, one of the numerous cities to be completely submerged by the Three Gorges Dam, as the site to continue his exploration of lost and found hometowns should not be read as a turn towards nihilism as much as the natural development of Jia's passion for capturing fleeting images of that soon to be lost.

Over the years, Jia has consistently extended his cinematic universe by repeatedly reintroducing actors, characters and sites from his earlier films. Such a strategy even extends beyond his own body of work, bleeding into the films of his collaborators, such as Liang Yonghao, the police officer in *Xiao Wu* and *Platform*, who reprised his role as a policeman in Han Jie's *Walk on the Wild Side* (2007) (which was produced by Jia and featured a cameo from Zhao Tao in a role quite similar to that of Qiaoqiao). At the same time, Jia has seemed to leave the question of any actual narrative continuity between his respective films intentionally open and ambiguous.

Still Life takes a similar approach, seemingly picking up one of the narrative lines left unexcavated from *Platform*. On the first stop of Cui Mingliang's journey beyond the city walls of Fenyang in *Platform* he meets his cousin Sanming, the silent mine worker victimised by poverty and exploitation. During a visit to Sanming's home, his mother explains the difficulties of finding her son a wife to Cui Mingliang.

Later, while sitting on a mountain ridge overlooking a vast expanse of hills and mines, Sanming shows Cui Mingliang the photo of a mysterious woman – she is never identified and there is no further narrative exposition on her origins. But six years later (and more than sixteen years later in narrative film time), Jia Zhangke offers a possible explanation via his 2006 award-winning film *Still Life*. In *Still Life* Sanming returns, venturing from Fenyang to Fengjie in search of his wife (the mysterious woman in the photo he shows Cui Mingliang in Platform?) amid the ruins of a city on the brink of

being submerged. The tale of undoing unfolds on many levels, as the original hometown (Fenyang) is forsaken, the new hometown (Fengjie) is destroyed and family ties are broken, seemingly never to be renewed – once the floodwaters rise, there is no going back.[83]

Sanming gazes out over the remains of Fengjie as the floodwaters rise and we are reminded of that almost identical scene shot nearly a decade earlier in *Platform* when Sanming looked out on the ridge overlooking rural Fenyang just after signing his life away to the mine. The stretch of land Sanming stared out at in *Platform* was the coal country of Shanxi. Now, all these years later, unfurling before his eyes is the soon-to-be wasteland, or waterland, of Fengjie. Both represent equally haunting images of environmental devastation laid to waste along the path of China's modernisation. Though the mines of Fenyang have torn open the earth from the inside out and the great dam will leave Fengjie completely submerged beneath the waters of the Yangtze, emerging from the shell of these cities is the fossil fuel and hydroelectric power that will drive China's economic miracle. So while Jia's characters are repeatedly alienated from their *physical* surroundings, it is the new world of materialist desires and Coca-Cola dreams emerging from the ruins that will provide the *spiritual* alienation that will further haunt Xiao Wu, Cui Mingliang,

Sanming at the mines outside Fenyang (*Platform*): gazing out over the desolate landscape

Binbin, Xiao Ji and Sanming in their cyclical struggle with the reality of their environment and the new manufactured ideals that arise from its ashes.

Returning to *Still Life*, it is only towards the end of the film that we are presented with a moral twist that problematises the simple, tragic figure of Sanming – who spends the film stubbornly searching the ruins of a soon-to-be-lost city for his missing family. It becomes clear that the happy, homogeneous family Sanming searches for probably never even existed – it is revealed that Sanming's wife was *purchased* for 3,000 yuan, a victim of human trafficking. With the hometown destroyed and relationships in shambles, Jia seems to leave us with a dark and bitter postscript for his 'Hometown Trilogy' and cinematic search for home. (As Xi Chuan has noted the complex dimensions of Sanming's marriage are further conflated when we realise the deep emotional and familial links that remain between Sanming and his estranged wife.[84]) But once the hometown has been abandoned, destroyed or submerged, what is left? Perhaps the answer already lies in Jia's 2005 film *The World* where the characters find themselves trapped between an artificial world of model reproductions of historic

Sanming in Fengjie (*Still Life*): between piles of rubble in the foreground and rising waters in the background

cultural sites and the virtual world of mobile phones and digital reality.

While this study began with Xiao Shan's desire to leave Beijing and return to Shanxi, with *The World* Jia's protagonists find themselves back in Beijing working in World Park, a theme park modelled on the Epcot Center where all of the great tourist sites of the world are collected in miniature. There migrant workers from Fenyang and beyond can have lunch atop the Eiffel Tower, stroll over London Bridge and gaze at the World Trade Center Towers, which, as one character observes, here are still standing. *The World* features not only a scathing critique of globalism, a meditation on the place of simulacrum in postmodern society and a probing take on post-socialist alienation, but also places Jia's 'Hometown Trilogy' in a completely new context. With *The World*, it seems the hometown (the local) has finally been forsaken for the world (the global), or at least its image.

The New World: from the Leaning Tower of Pisa to Manhattan in Jia Zhangke's *The World*

6 Appendix: In Conversation with Jia Zhangke

The following interview was conducted with Jia Zhangke on 30 September 2002 in New York. Jia was attending the New York Film Festival with Chow Keung, where *Unknown Pleasures*, the third and final instalment of his trilogy, was screening. This excerpt focuses on Jia's 'Hometown Trilogy', covering a variety of topics, from his use of popular music to experience with non-professional actors and from cinematography to the images of destruction that run through his work.

Michael Berry: Music plays a very important role in all of your films. It can represent the passage of time, means of communicating, or a kind of cultural symbol. From karaoke, opera and Canto-pop to rock 'n' roll, hummed melodies and musical cigarette lighters, music seems an ever-present motif and carries a subtle yet awesome power in your characters' lives and your cinematic narratives.

Jia Zhangke: I have always loved music. Even when I was in college I once wrote a thesis essay on the relationship between film narrative and music. I feel that there are all kinds of structural aspects to music that can be incorporated into a narrative. So even then I was already playing around with these rather abstract thoughts about the relationship between music and film. In the years preceding the shooting of *Xiao Wu* karaoke became extremely popular in China. I went with a bunch of friends to a karaoke club in my hometown where we saw a guy all alone who kept singing the same songs over and over again. His voice was really terrible and at first I found him annoying but as time went by and I watched him sing I suddenly found myself quite moved. That experience really made me look at popular culture in a new light. In such a cold and difficult environment [popular culture] provides a place to come home to, it serves as a means of providing self-comfort. So it was really that experience that led to all of those karaoke scenes in *Xiao Wu*.

Another factor stems from the fact that I was born in 1970, so I was in my formative years in the early 1980s when popular music really began to take root in China. So I really grew up with pop music. Popular music really played an enormous role in the lives of people of my generation as we matured and came of age. At first it was all popular music from Hong Kong and Taiwan, and only later did western music start coming into China. One of the reasons [popular music] was so important was because previous to this China really didn't have any 'popular culture' to speak of. The closest thing we had were revolutionary model operas and things made in that mould. I still remember so clearly the first time I heard the music of Teresa Teng (Deng Lijun); the experience was exactly as it was portrayed in *Platform*, where the characters listened to illegal short-wave radio broadcasts from Taiwan. At the time, I was quite young and couldn't really say what it was about her voice, but it was so moving – I was utterly hypnotised. There was a special time every day when they would play her songs and I would always tune in.

Later when I went to college and reflected back on this time I realised that her music represented a massive change in our cultural landscape. When I was a child we used to always sing 'We Carry On Communism' ('Women shi gongchanzhuyi de jiebanren') or in the 1980s we sung 'We are the New Generation of the 1980s' ('Women shi bashi niandai de xin yidai'), both of which highlighted 'we' – the collective. But Teresa Teng's songs were always about 'me' – the individual. Songs like 'I Love You' ('Wo ai ni') and 'The Moon Represents My Heart' ('Yueliang daibiao wo de xin') were something completely new. So people of my generation were suddenly infected with this very personal individual world. Before that everything was collective, we lived in a collective dormitory, our parents worked as part of a collective and our schools were structured in the same manner. In our educational system the individual belonged to the nation and was part of the collective. But in the 1980s everything changed and it all started with popular music.

This is especially evident in *Platform* where I tried to consciously inject all the music that moved me over the years into the film. So there is a historicity immediately built into the narrative through the music. There are also several specific songs that really represent what the Chinese people were going through during a given historical frame. For instance, in 1980 with the beginning of the Open Door policy when the government was trying to encourage the people about the optimistic future ahead there appeared an incredibly popular song entitled 'Young Friends Come Together' ('Nianqing de pengyou lai xianghui'). The key lines in the song are,

> In twenty years we will realise the Four Modernisations
> We will come together then and the world will be a beautiful place.

This song represented a kind of promise from the country to its people that the future will be brighter and tomorrow will be a better day. During the early days of the Open Door policy practically every young person in China was singing that song. They were filled with excitement and hope. By 1986 or 1987 we start getting songs like 'Go With Your Feelings' ('Gen zhe ganjue zuo'), which came during the initial thawing out period [after the Cultural Revolution] when we saw the beginning of free thought and expression. And then later came Cui Jian's anthem, 'I Have Nothing to My Name' ('Yiwu suoyou'). Each of these songs really represents a snapshot of the social reality of the time. So for a director of my generation I really cannot escape the influence of popular music, it is everywhere. There is a historical reason why these songs move us.

MB: Besides music, popular culture in general seems to have a incredible power in your films, but it is a power that is alternately both liberating and oppressive.

JZK: It is only natural for these to be a kind of oppressive component at work. When there is all of a sudden a voice that is telling people to start paying attention to their personal desires there is bound to be this kind of phenomena. For instance, loneliness; I have no doubt that in the 1960s and 1970s the Chinese people were often very lonely, but at the time they didn't know what loneliness meant. People then also had feelings of loneliness and desperation but they would never feel that those were natural human emotions. Only once our minds were liberated and we started paying attention to ourselves as individuals and began to read Freud, Nietzsche,

Schopenhaur and other forms of western thought and philosophy did we begin to understand ourselves, and with that came a kind of loneliness and desperation. But this is all actually a very natural phenomena.

MB: As your first feature film, what led you to centre *Xiao Wu* around the story of a pickpocket? Growing up in Fenyang, did you know people like Xiao Wu?

JZK: Before getting to work on *Xiao Wu* I had originally wanted to do a short about a man and a woman and their first night together. I wanted to make it a short film that featured one locale (a bedroom), one temporal space (a single night) and just two characters. We were getting ready to shoot and my

Jia Zhangke outside Alice Tully Hall during one of the first international screenings of *Unknown Pleasures* at the New York Film Festival, 2002

cinematographer Yu Lik Wai came in from Hong Kong. Spring Festival was just around the corner and it had been a full year since I had been home so I went back to Fenyang. When I arrived I was suddenly struck by how dramatically the city had changed in just one year. The rate of Fenyang's modernisation and economic growth, not to mention the impact the forces of commodification had on people there, were all unbelievable. Shanxi is already a backwater province, relatively, in China and Fenyang, being on the bank of the Yellow River and close to Shaanxi, makes it a rather remote place even in Shanxi, so the fact that these changes were reaching even Fenyang and in such a visible way had an incredible impact on me. The changes stunned me, especially when I discovered that so many old friends of mine were no longer even speaking to one another. I also had several friends who, after getting married, were starting to have problems with their parents and barely spoke to them. Then there were friends who had just got married and were now already divorced. I just felt that people were changing so quickly, everything was a blur. All in the course of year it seemed as if all of those interpersonal relationships and friendships I had were completely transformed.

Then there was the sudden development of countless karaoke clubs and karaoke girls – who were basically prostitutes – all of this became so commonplace. There was an ancient road near the neighbourhood where I grew up and that entire road was to be torn down, just like the scene portrayed in *Xiao Wu*. All of this radical change playing out right there before my eyes left me with a pressing urge to shoot it and capture it before it was gone. The interior of China was amid this massive transformation – not on the eve of great change or just after great change – it was all happening right there. I knew it might not last long, perhaps one year, maybe two, but it was a time of immense pain. So amid this excitement I decided to make a movie about an ordinary Chinese man living amid this environment of upheaval and massive social change.

Another reason for why I decided to make *Xiao Wu* was that in 1997 I was getting ready to graduate from the Beijing Film Academy and, after four years of watching Chinese films, I still hadn't seen a single Chinese film that had anything to do with the Chinese reality that I knew. After the Fifth Generation's initial success, their artistic works started to undergo a lot of changes. One of these big changes came with Chen Kaige, who once said that, 'I increasingly feel that film should be used as a vehicle to describe legend.' I, however, could not disagree more. Sure film can describe legend, but where is it written that film can't depict other things as well? Unfortunately, most of the Fifth Generation directors all followed this trajectory. Moreover, it became increasingly common to see Fifth Generation directors imitating each other. For instance Huang Jianxin, who I am very fond of, made a film called *The Wooden Man's Bride (Wukui)* (1993), He Ping also did a film in this style called *Red Firecracker, Green Firecracker (Pao da shuang deng)* (1994). These kinds of imaginary representations of traditional Chinese society became increasingly common [after the success of similar period pieces by directors like Chen Kaige and Zhang Yimou]. But there was a very clear disconnect between these films and the current Chinese reality that we were living in. There is something about this phenomena that left me feeling very unsatisfied and it was partially out of this frustration that I decided to make films. I told my collaborators at the time that I wanted to express the here and the now (*dangxia xing*) in my films, and that has been the aim of our films ever since. Although *Xiao Wu* was made in 1997, today China still faces many of the same problems and exists in a state of agony, brought on by its current state of massive change and transformation. For an artist this can be a double-edged sword because, on the one hand, living in this environment of constant change can generate a lot of creative inspiration, especially with the camera; however, the other side of the coin is the multitude of problems brought on by this change and all of the hardships the people must go through in this process.

MB: So although you grew up in Fenyang and shooting there must have been a homecoming of sorts, there was also a kind of alienation after having been away during this time of rapid change?

JZK: Right, the transformation of Fenyang is really incredible. So, whenever I go back, part of me feels like a stranger. For instance, the means by which young people today communicate with each other and get along is really completely different from what it was. This really showed me how to capture the transformation of my surroundings with a kind of sensitivity, which should always be the responsibility of a director. Naturally, there are some directors who neglect reality in their work, but my aesthetic taste and goals don't allow me to do that – I can never escape reality. So, in *Unknown Pleasures*, I made a film about a younger generation with different values and characteristics than my generation. Growing up I always played with at least three or four other kids, often all the kids on the block played together – the power of the collective was extremely strong and culturally speaking we always had a lot of confidence. But the younger generation are faced with a new kind of cultural oppression. This is in part due to the lifestyles they hear and learn about through the media – especially the internet and cable television – which exists on a completely different plane from their everyday reality. It is this radical contrast between the reality of their environment and the picture of the world they get through the media that creates an enormous pressure in their lives.

We completed *Xiao Wu* in just twenty-one shooting days and a big part of my goal was to capture relationships in transformation. Chinese people live in a world where they are dependent on interpersonal relationships. Whether they be family relationships, friendships, husband–wife relations, we are always living in the context and confines of a relationship. And describing the structure of these relationships was really what I wanted to express through *Xiao Wu*. So the first section of the film is about the relationship between two friends. Within this relationship there is a fundamental change brought on by broken promises and the loss of trust that the friendship was once based upon. The second section of the film is about love and Xiao Wu's relationship with Meimei. In the past the Chinese view of love was always an eternal one, from now until forever – the relationship between Xiao Wu and Meimei, however, is only about the moment, the now. Fate is destined to tear them apart. The final section is about family and the relationship with one's parents, another source of many problems. Of all the radical changes confronting the Chinese people in recent years I feel the most fundamental and devastating change is in interpersonal relationships.

MB: In one sense, it is as if all the characters are wearing a mask, pretending to be someone they are not. Xiaoyong, once a thief, is now a model entrepreneur; Meimei calls herself a karaoke girl while she works as a prostitute and her parents think she is studying acting in Beijing . . .

JZK: Right, that's something I wanted to express. In China there are two kinds of people: those who can adapt to the changes around them, like Xiaoyong, Xiao Wu's childhood friend. In the film he takes part in all kinds of illegal activities, like importing contraband cigarettes, but he describes himself as 'being in business'. He uses a word game to completely alleviate any moral burden or responsibility. Another example is when he opens up a dance hall, which is actually a place for prostitution; he says 'I'm in the entertainment industry.' He has the power to cover up his behaviour with language. He knows how to adapt to his environment, unlike Xiao Wu who is helpless in this regard. Take, for example, his profession; for Xiao Wu a thief is a thief. There is nothing he can say or do to change his inferior moral position. This is further augmented by his idealised view of friendship and interpersonal relationships.

MB: *Platform* is considered by many critics to be one of the greatest films of contemporary Chinese cinema; let's talk a bit about the inception of *Platform*. You actually started writing the screenplay in 1995 before *Xiao Wu*?

JZK: Right. *Platform* was the first full-length script I wrote and it was completed long before *Xiao Wu* was even conceived. While I was still working on my shorts I kept asking myself what I should do for my first full-length feature film, should I get the chance to make one. What I came up with was *Platform*, the 1980s, popular culture. For me, as well as most Chinese, the 1980s was an unforgettable decade in China. The move towards materialism was shocking. When I was seven or eight I remember hearing a guy a few years older than me say, 'If one day I can buy a motorcycle, I'd be the happiest man on Earth!' At the time the only people who could have a motorcycle were postmen and policemen; for everyone else owning a motorcycle was an unthinkable luxury. So for him the happiest thing in the world would be having a motorcycle. But less than three or four years later the streets of China were already filled with motorcycles. Television is another example. As a child we would go to governmental offices like the meeting hall at the labour union, where hundreds of people would all cram together to watch one TV, but just two or three years later virtually every family had their own television set. I remember how shocked I was the first time I learned what a washing machine was. There was a segment about washing machines during a school screening of an educational film called *The New Face of China* (*Zuguo xinmao*) (1983), which introduced all kinds of new architecture and products in China – two years later my parents brought home a washing machine. So the rate of material growth and change in China during that period was extremely fast.

The other aspect of this change is spiritual. When I was little there were few books available and exposure to outside cultures was strictly limited. But the thaw happened quickly and, by 1983 or 1984, even in a remote place like Fenyang you could buy books by Freud and Nietzsche. I didn't really understand what they were writing about, but was nonetheless ecstatic to be able to read them (laughs). The change was incredible and the entire decade of the 1980s was one filled with idealism and excitement. Everyone believed that the future would be bright. People started to gain a newfound power, but all of this met with a great setback in 1989, which proved to have huge consequences for all Chinese people. Only after 1989 did people truly start to attain a new kind of independent lifestyle. Take myself, for example; according to the official system I don't have a work unit or a job. People used to think that you could only be a normal part of society if you belonged to a work unit, but all of that changed after 1989. Suddenly there was the birth of a whole group of independent intellectuals and artists. Private capital gradually became available and we made the commitment to take the independent route outside of the official system. The same goes for independent/underground film in China, which really did not start to develop until after 1989 with film-makers like Zhang Yuan. This is what the 1980s culture left us with. So looking back at the 1980s I could not control my excitement and decided that I wanted to make a film about the 1980s. The problem was how to portray this period and what I came up with was using a song and dance troupe (*wengong tuan*) to reflect that period. Song and dance troupes are at the bottom of the totem pole among cultural workers in China and from their transformation we can see the transformation of all of China.

MB: Were you a member of a song and dance troupe?

JZK: Not an actual member, but I participated in a lot of performances. In high school we saw an American movie called *Breakin'*.[85] I must have watched that movie ten, twenty times, and learned all the moves from that movie. I became a breakdancer.

MB: Can you still breakdance?

JZK: Oh yeah! (laughs) It was right about this time that song and dance troupes were cut off from state financing and had to tour poor provincial areas to sustain themselves economically. Since I could breakdance, they often took me on tour during my summer vacations, adding a breakdance showcase to the performance. In addition to my experience, my older sister was also a violinist with a song and dance troupe in the early 1980s. It was a combination of these two experiences that inspired the film.

Once the script was written I started negotiations with my Hong Kong producers about a full-length feature film. At the time, however, the available funding was extremely limited and I felt that *Platform* would require a larger investment to accurately recreate the historical background and cover the expenses of all the travel (since the film is about a touring troupe). All we had was 200,000 yuan and there was no way to shoot *Platform* on that small amount, so we went ahead and shot *Xiao Wu* first. After the success of *Xiao Wu* funding came easier; suddenly there many international producers interested in working with us. In the end we decided to collaborate with Shozo Ichiyama from Japan. A main factor in my decision to work with Shozo was the fact that he had produced Hou Hsiao-hsien's *Goodbye South, Goodbye* (*Nanguo zaijian, nanguo*) (1996) and *Flowers of Shanghai* (*Haishang hua*) (1998). Hou Hsiao-hsien is a director I have greatly admired for many years so I felt that, based on Shozo's relationship with Hou, we should be able to understand each other artistically. He came on to produce *Platform* and he indeed turned out to be a wonderful producer.

MB: Is it a fair assessment to say that *Platform* is the most personal of your works? Or even autobiographical?

JZK: I would agree with that. Naturally there are a lot of differences between the characters depicted and myself, they are actually about ten years older than me. But several scenes in *Platform* are derived from things I saw growing up and the latter half of the film was even influenced heavily by my own experiences.

MB: How did you discover your lead actor, Wang Hongwei? What is it about his performance and acting style that attracted you initially to him and led you to continually recast him?

JZK: Wang Hongwei was a classmate of mine in college. We were both Film Theory majors. When I made *Xiao Shan Goes Home,* he played the role of Xiao Shan. I really admire his work. One thing that initially attracted me to him was the plainness of his appearance, his face looks just like countless other Chinese people.

MB: And *Xiao Shan Going Home* was his first film as an actor?

JZK: Yes, that was his first film.[86] What really attracted me to him as an actor is his sensitivity and self-respect.

MB: What is interesting is that although your first films end with the shockingly powerful credit, 'This film was made with non-professional actors', by the time we get to *Unknown Pleasures* Wang Hongwei in the role of Xiao Wu is a kind of cultural icon, which you playfully reference.

JZK: Right. He has changed and on one level is already a cultural symbol of sorts, which we see towards the end when he tries to purchase bootleg copies of *Xiao Wu* and *Platform*.

MB: Besides Wang, another core member of your creative team is Yu Lik Wai.[87] A brilliant cinematographer and a director in his own right, Yu has a very unique style that juxtaposes jarring hand-held work reminiscent of Christopher Doyle with steady long takes in the spirit of Hou Hsiao-hsien's works. Could you talk about your working relationship with Yu?

JZK: My working relationship with Yu Lik Wai began in Hong Kong at the Hong King Independent Film Festival when I saw a documentary he directed entitled *Neon Goddesses.* I really admired his cinematic approach and felt that it was extremely close to what I was going for in my own work. We started to talk and hit it off right from the bat. I remember during our first conversation I mentioned the French director Robert Bresson. I never imagined that Bresson was also one of Yu's favourite film-makers, so immediately there was this instant connection. We got on so well that we started collaborating almost immediately and made three films together. One critic in China described our collaborative relationship as perfect partners in crime. (laughs) One of the main differences between our collaboration is that we're not just business partners, but also very close friends. We see each other almost every day and usually before my next screenplay is even written he already knows exactly what it is about because I'm constantly sharing my ideas with him. So on-set there isn't much need for communication because he already knows what I'm after.

MB: So in some way Yu Lik Wai is your most important collaborator.

JZK: Without question. A good director really needs a very strong cinematographer by his side to support him. His vocabulary of visuals is what supports my aesthetic vision. I have seen a lot of films made by my fellow film-makers and I always feel it is such a shame to see films by directors with vision who lack the visual support they need. Naturally, there is a lot of room for aesthetic critique of the Fifth Generation directors, but one reason for their overall success is that they all have an incredibly strong visual support team; people like Gu Changwei and Zhang Yimou have such a strong aesthetic sense. In my graduating class at the Beijing Film Academy we had a lot of cinematography majors, but there really wasn't anyone that I felt was speaking the same aesthetic language as myself. But as soon as I saw Yu Lik Wai's *Neon Goddesses* I instantly realised that he was someone I should collaborate with. What's funny is that after seeing my film, he also wanted to work with me. So it is was very interesting the way everything came about, as if it was all meant to be.

MB: All of your films employ large numbers of non-professional actors, what are some of the pros and cons of using non-professional actors?

JZK: I have been using non-professional actors in my films ever since my early shorts. This really has to do with my current aesthetic taste and my desire to make films about people in a very natural and realistic state. Professional actors have all undergone extended speech training and long periods of study on how to act with their bodies. So it is very difficult to adapt their methods of movement and speech into the kind of documentary-esque type of narrative film I am making. An actor trained in body movement is bound to stick out when walking down the streets of a place like Fenyang, it is extremely difficult to get them to fit in with their surrounding environment. So the benefit of using non-professional actors is that their speech and movements are extremely natural.

The other reason is that non-professional actors can really understand what I am trying to express with the script. Since they grew up in a very similar atmosphere they can believe in the script, they believe in the characters and their universe. For instance, the actors we used in *Xiao Wu* and *Platform* grew up in that very environment. We would shoot scenes on streets that they had been walking back and forth on for twenty or thirty years, so they all had a natural confidence and 'at home' feeling with which professional actors can't compare.

Non-professional actors also provide me with a lot of inspiration, especially in the linguistic realm. In my scripts, dialogues are basically just a rough blueprint with ample room for development. I always leave it up to the individual actors to choose their own words to express what is on the page. Let me give you an example. There is scene in *Platform* where the girl who used to be a dancer is doing a scene with Zhong Ping where they are both smoking. So before we began to shoot I explained the scene to her and told her, 'You just came in from the street to tell her that Zhang Jun has gone to Guangzhou.' So she walked in and said, 'Hey they're parading some criminals down the street!' As soon as I heard this I was so moved. Back in the early 1980s it used to be quite common to see sentenced criminals paraded down the streets of Fenyang for public exhibition. Her creativity in throwing in this line was something completely inspired by her experience of growing up in the streets of Fenyang. These moments of spontaneous creativity added so much to the film, really making it come alive. If I had used a professional actor, on the other hand, they probably would never have added anything like that because they have no idea what went on in the streets of Fenyang during that era. It is details like this that really added so much subtle colour to *Platform*.

MB: And the challenges?

JZK: Well, at the same time there are also a lot of complications involved with non-professional actors due to their unfamiliarity with the art. It takes a lot of work to help them build up confidence in the characters they are playing. For example, if I ask a non-professional actress to play a woman going for an abortion, she will often have a prejudice to playing such a role. Or if I want her to perform a certain dance, she will ask why. All of this requires extra effort on the part of the director. The link between the director and non-professional actors is very vulnerable and demands a lot of time and attention. Unlike professional actors, who basically have a professional working relationship with the director, non-professionals require you to build up friendship and trust. If the actor loses this trust in the director there is basically no hope of inducing a genuine performance. So the whole process takes a lot of time. Another factor coming into play here is the spontaneous style with which I make films, which tends to influence the rhythm of the work. Often an actor will deliver lines spontaneously during shooting and, although the words are incredible, it sometimes gets too long making the scene go over and influencing the rhythm of the film. Gradually, however, I am figuring out ways to deal with these types of problems. After all, that's what film is about – it's all based on experience.

MB: Although some directors are turning to digital as a less expensive alternative to celluloid, there remain questions about the feasibility of a true digital revolution due to the technical and aesthetic limitations of the medium, as well as the complications associated with transferring work shot in digital to traditional film stock. Since its release, however, critics have been calling *Unknown Pleasures* the most successful film ever shot with DV technology.

JZK: Actually, I feel that there are a lot of problems with *Unknown Pleasures*. One problem was that in the process of resolving some of the problems associated with shooting in digital we sacrificed a lot. For instance, we cut back heavily on exterior shots due to the poor quality of filming in the sunlight. Another problem was with the different camera lengths, some of which were too large for me to utilise – so there are some restrictions when working with digital. But working in digital was really a new experience and I found that there was much less pressure on the shoot. It was a very relaxed atmosphere and we had the freedom to experiment with lots of different things.

For instance, the second to last scene in *Unknown Pleasures* when the character Xiao Ji is riding his motorcycle down the highway – that whole scene is purely the result of digital. In the scene Xiao Ji's bike starts to stall and suddenly it begins to thunder and it rains – the whole comes together beautifully as if the environment is complementing his internal feelings. Actually that scene had already been finished and we were packing up for the day when the sky suddenly grew dark and it looked like it was going to pour. Now if I had been making a traditional film I would have just told everyone to pack it up and go home for the day, after all we already had a good take. But since we were shooting in digital there was no pressure, we were completely free, so I suggested one more take. That final take was the one we used in the film [with the rain].

Digital film also seems to bring a certain degree of abstractness when shooting in public spaces. This required some readjustment on my side because when I was first experimenting with digital video my impression was that the medium would bring a new life to public spaces, but actually the result was an abstract quality. Every space has a kind of abstract order. Traditional film works to break up this order, making people appear active and excited, but digital interacts with its subjects in a very quiet way enabling me to capture a cold, distant, almost abstract quality. This is something I realised a few days after shooting and adjusted to fit the story. Actually it works quite well for a film about lost youth like this.

MB: Let's talk a moment about the place of destruction and ruins in your work. Towards the end of *Xiao Wu* an entire block is being torn down, but by the time we get to *Unknown Pleasures* it appears an entire city is in a state of utter ruins. Can you talk a bit about the politics of destruction in your work, from the destruction of youth or the destruction of locales?

JZK: There are definitely some connections between *Xiao Wu* and *Unknown Pleasures*; not only is there the cameo reappearance of the character Xiao Wu, but also there is the echoing of the motif of destruction. The entire city exists in a state of desolation. All of those old industrial factories have stopped production, leaving a cold, abandoned feeling that permeates the city. Datong left me with all kinds of feelings of desperation and devastation. In one sense it is truly a city in ruins and the people who inhabit the city very much live in a spiritual world that reflects their environment.

Notes

1 One alternate screening possibility for Chinese viewers came in the form of 'film clubs', which would organise small-scale screenings in bars, clubs and university classrooms in major cities.

2 Jia Zhangke has also written about his encounter with Martin Scorsese in the essay 'Wo de "zhangbei" Matian Shigaoxisi' ('My Eldership of Film' [sic]) in *City Magazine*, April 2006.

3 Yingjin Zhang, 'My Camera Doesn't Lie? Truth, Subjectivity, and Audience in Chinese Independent Film and Video', in Paul G. Pickowicz and Yingjin Zhang (eds), *From Underground to Independent: Alternative Film Culture in Contemporary China* (Lanham: Rowan & Littlefield, 2006), pp. 38–9.

4 In a 2006 forum, critic Cui Weiping declared that *Xiao Wu* and Chen Kaige's *Yellow Earth* stand as the two representative masterpieces of two eras of Chinese cinema in the reform era. See Cui's comments in Ouyang Jianghe (ed.), *On the Edge: Chinese Independent Cinema* (*Zhongguo duli dianying fangtanlu*) (Oxford: Oxford University Press, 2007), pp. 244–5.

5 Lin Xudong, Zhang Yaxuan and Gu Zheng, *Jia Zhangke dianying: Zhantai* (*The Films of Jia Zhangke:* Platform) (Beijing: Zhongguo mangwen chubanshe, 2003), p. 192.

6 Michael Berry, *Speaking in Images: Interviews with Contemporary Chinese Filmmakers* (New York: Columbia University Press, 2005), p. 185.

7 By all accounts, production of the three films were not explicitly planned as a trilogy. But in China the films were marketed together as the 'Hometown Trilogy' through a series of three book publications endorsed by the filmmakers and subsequent PRC DVD editions (many of which were bootleg) further marketed the films as a trilogy.

8 See Jonathan Rosenbaum's essay, 'Zhang Ke Jia, Poetic Prophet', which actually argues that Jia's small-town roots are a major part of what makes him such an exciting director, available at <www.jonathanrosenbaum.com/?p=7854> Kevin Lee's comments on his director profile for *Senses of Cinema* can be found online at <www.sensesofcinema.com/contents/directors/03/jia.html#4>

9 Ouyang Jianghe, *On the Edge*, p. 268.

10 Jin Liu has made a similar argument about Jia's ambition to have his hometown 'stand for China' in her article, 'The Rhetoric of Local Languages as the Marginal: Chinese Underground and Independent Films by Jia Zhangke and Others', *Modern Chinese Literature and Culture* vol. 18 no. 2, Autumn 2006, p. 179.

11 On 21 February 2006, before a screening of *Still Life* in Fenyang, Jia made the announcement that he hoped to shoot several more features in his hometown.

12 See Jason McGrath, 'The Independent Cinema of Jia Zhangke: From Postsocialist Realism to a Translational Aesthetic', in Zhang Zhen (ed.), *The Urban Generation: Chinese Cinema and Society at the Turn of the Twenty-first Century* (Durham: Duke University Press), pp. 81–114 and Wang Hui's comments in Ouyang Jianghe, *On* the Edge, p. 263. While McGrath identifies Jia's influences more broadly (but in a more comprehensive fashion), Wang's comments specifically point to the Underground Chinese Documentary Film Movement and the international art films of Hou Hsiao-hsien and Ozu Yasujiro as the primary powers at work in the formation of Jia's aesthetic. Kent Jones may have been the first to directly link the influence of Hou and Ozu on Jia in his article 'Out of Time', Film Comment vol. 38 no. 5, 2002, pp. 43–7, although Jia himself has singled out the influence of Ozu and Hou in numerous interviews, such as Stephen Teo's 2001 interview, 'Cinema with an Accent', in Senses of Cinema, available at <www.sensesofcinema.com/contents/01/15/zhangke_interview.html>

13 Curse of the Golden Flower and Still Life were both released on 14 December 2006. The tag line attached to the latter film was 'In the age of gold worshippers, who still cares about good people?'; the 'gold' referencing Zhang's film, while 'good people' referred to Sanxia haoren, the Chinese title of Still Life. On 5 December, Jia told a reporter from Morning News that 'the Fifth Generation has no ability make big budget commercial films'.

14 Robert Bresson (1901–1999) was a painter and film director who became a key figure in French cinema. After beginning making films in 1934, Bresson directed thirteen feature films over the course of more than four decades. His major works include A Man Escaped, Pickpocket, Diary of a Country Priest and The Trial of Joan of Arc.

15 Although Yu would go on to shoot all of Jia's subsequent films, he would also direct more of his own independent features, including Love Will Tear Us Apart and All Tomorrow's Parties in addition to working on other films as a cinematographer, including Wong Kar-wai's In the Mood for Love.

16 Lin Xudong, Zhang Yaxuan and Gu Zheng, Jia Zhangke dianying: Zhantai, p. 195.

17 Ouyang Jianghe, On the Edge, pp. 260–1.

18 Zhang Xianmin, Invisible Images (Kanbujian de yingxiang) (Shanghai: Shanghai San lian, 2004), p. 40.

19 Lin Xudong, Zhang Yaxuan and Gu Zheng, Jia Zhangke dianying: Ren xiaoyao (The Films of Jia Zhangke: Unknown Pleasures) (Beijing: Zhongguo mangwen chubanshe, 2003), pp. 116–17.

20 Stephen Teo, 'Cinema with an Accent', in Senses of Cinema, available at <www.sensesofcinema.com/contents/01/15/zhangke_interview.html>

21 Chris Berry, 'Xiao Wu: Watching Time Go By', in Chris Berry (ed.), Chinese Films in Focus II (London: BFI, 2008), p. 252.

22 Jia spoke of this incident with Lin Xiaoling in an interview with Sun Jianmin. See Jiang Yuanlun and Shi Jian (eds), Xianfeng, Duihua: Women yijing xuanze (Avant-Garde Dialogues: We Have Already Chosen) (Guilin: Guangxi Normal University Press, 2004), p. 22.

23 Kevin Lee, 'Jia Zhangke', available at <www.sensesofcinema.com/contents/directors/03/jia.html#4>

24 Of course, some characters, such as Meimei and the Madame at the karaoke club/brothel where she works, speak Mandarin.

25 For an insightful discussion of the tensions playing out between diegesis and mimesis in the soundtracks and dialects of Jia's films, see Jin Liu, 'The Rhetoric of Local Languages as the Marginal', pp. 163–205. Liu also explores similar dialect issues in *Platform* where none of the four main actors speak the Fenyang dialect where their characters purportedly grew up.

26 Xiaoping Lin, 'Jia Zhangke's Cinematic Trilogy: A Journey across the Ruins of Post-Mao China', in Sheldon H. Lu and Emilie Yueh-yu Yeh (eds), *Chinese-Language Film: Historiography, Poetics, Politics* (Honolulu: University of Hawaii Press, 2005), p. 191.

27 Berry, *Speaking in Images*, p. 202.

28 Ibid.

29 Jiang Yuanlun and Shi Jian, *Xianfeng, Duihua*, p. 35.

30 Cui Shuqin, 'Negotiating In-Between: On New-generation Filmmaking and Jia Zhangke's Films', *Modern Chinese Literature and Culture* vol 18 no. 2, Auturm 2006, p. 110.

31 Xiaoping Lin has also written about the central place of 'gift exchange' in the film and the way in which failure of such exchanges signifies a fundamental breakdown of traditional agrarian 'gift economy'. See Xiaoping Lin, 'Jia Zhangke's Cinematic Trilogy'.

32 This is illustrated by the couplet of tattoos on his and Xiaoyong's arms.

33 The film-makers only changed the title of the film to *Xiao Wu* or *The*

Pickpocket for marketing and distribution considerations. The original title was simply too long.

34 Lin Xudong, Zhang Yaxuan and Gu Zheng, *Jia Zhangke dianying: Xiao Wu (The Films of Jia Zhangke: Xiao Wu)* (Beijing: Zhongguo mangwen chubanshe, 2003), p. 107.

35 For more on the seemingly unquenchable appetite for revisiting the story of Ah Q in modern China, see Paul Foster, *Ah Q Archaeology: Lu Xun, Ah Q Progeny and the National Character Discourse in Twentieth-Century China* (Lanham: Lexington Books, 2006).

36 Lu Xun, *Selected Stories* (New York: W. W. Norton, 2003), p. 67.

37 If we pursue the Ah Q symmetry further, the earlier discussed bathhouse scene where Xiao Wu is also and in his own world could even be read as a parallel to Ah Q's fantastic dream sequence from Fan Cen's 1981 film adaptation of the story.

38 Berry, *Speaking in Images*, p. viii.

39 Chris Berry has noted a resonance with an alternate scene at the beginning of the film involving the protagonist, which creates another level of framing. 'The film, which began with a young man waiting by the side of the road, followed by another young man waiting then boarding a bus, ends with that same young man chained to the side of the road. Like the young man in the first shot of the credits sequence, Xiao Wu squats down by the side of the road, and looks about.' See Berry, '*Xiao Wu*', p. 251.

40 Lu Xun (1881–1936), the father of modern Chinese literature, gave up a career in medicine and began writing after seeing a slide of a Chinese man being executed who was surrounded by a crowd of his compatriots who looked on numbly as the sentence was passed. Images of apathetic crowds would later be featured prominately in several of Lu Xun's later literary works such as 1921's *The True Story of Ah Q (Ah Q zhengzhuan)*.

41 Berry, *Speaking in Images*, p. 203.

42 Although Xiao Wu is portrayed in earnest in *Xiao Wu*, his character makes a cameo in 2002's *Unknown Pleasures* and is very much portrayed in an ironic, almost comic fashion as he tries purchasing bootleg copies of *Xiao Wu* from one of the film's protagonists.

43 Rosenbaum and Hoberman's quotes appear on the New Yorker Video release of *Platform*. Hoberman, in particular, has given the film high praise, writing of *Platform* in the 21 February 2001 edition of the *Chicago Reader*, 'might be the greatest film ever to come out of mainland China'. 'Please Watch Carefully: The Heart of the World', available at <http://www.chicagoreader.com/movies/archives/2001/0102/010223.html>

44 Kang Xingxuan and Chen Fang, 'I Believe in the Cultural Value of My Films' ('Wo xiangxin ziji de dianying wenhua jiazhi'), *Ming Pao Monthly*, December 2006, p. 72.

45 Lin Xudong, Zhang Yaxuan and Gu Zheng, *Jia Zhangke dianying: Zhantai*, p. 191.

46 Stephen Teo, 'Cinema with an Accent', in *Senses of Cinema*, available at <www.sensesofcinema.com/contents/01/15/zhangke_interview.html>

47 Cheng Qingsong and Huang Ou, *Wo de sheyingji bu sahuang: xianfeng dianying ren dangan – shengya 1961–1970* (*My Camera Doesn't Lie*) (Beijing: Zhongguo youji chuban, 2002), p. 346.

48 For more on the different editions of *Platform*, see the short essay 'A Tale of Two Versions', which is included in the liner notes for the 2005 New Yorker Video release of the film.

49 In an interview with Sun Jianmin, Jia stated, 'I am about to begin shooting my second feature film *Platform*, which will be the twenty-year story of a local touring song and dance troupe between the years 1979 and 1999.' See Jiang Yuanlun and Shi Jian, *Xianfeng, Duihua*, p. 48.

50 Cui Shuqin, 'Negotiating In-Between', p. 123.

51 McGrath, 'The Independent Cinema of Jia Zhangke', p. 100.

52 Dennis Rea, *Live at the Forbidden City: Musical Encounters in China & Taiwan* (Lincoln, NE: iUniverse, 2007) p. 79.

53 Ibid., p. 80.

54 Cheng Qingsong and Huang Ou, *Wo de sheyingji bu sahuang*, p. 370.

55 McGrath, 'The Independent Cinema of Jia Zhangke', p. 98.

56 Ban Wang has written about the ways in which *Platform* challenges various conceptions of epic narrative. See Ban Wang, 'Epic Narrative, Authenticity, and the Memory of Realism: Reflections on Jia Zhangke's *Platform*', in Ching Kwan Lee and Guobin Yang (eds), *Re-envisioning the Chinese Revolution: The Politics and Poetics of*

Collective Memories in Reform China (Stanford: Stanford University Press, 2007), pp. 193–216 .

57 For more on *Awāra*, see Gayatri Chatterjee's award-winning book-length study, Awāra (New Delhi: Penguin Books India, 2003).

58 Cui Shuqin, 'Negotiating In-Between', pp. 118–19.

59 The popular Chinese translation of the lyrics was somewhat different, with the main chorus rendered as '*Daochu liulang, daochu liulang! Mingyun huan wo benxiang yuanfang, benxiang yuanfang!*', which could be literally translated as, 'Roaming aimlessly all about, roaming aimlessly all about! Fate has called on me to run away to a place far away, run far, far away!' The song was extremely popular in China during the 1950s, especially among teenage boys, and is said to have been of favourite of Chairman Mao himself.

60 Yoshihiro Hanno actually composed a forty-minute score for the film, but Jia only used a single fifteen-second motif, which appears three times in the film.

61 Xiaoping Lin, 'Jia Zhangke's Cinematic Trilogy', p. 199.

62 This scene also marks a visual demarcation line between the first half of the film set in Fenyang and the latter half which traces the reform era as the troupe traverse China. In order to emphasise this historical shift, Nelson Yu Lik Wai also employed a distinct visual strategy for the second half of the film. Whereas the first half employed primarily extended fixed camera sequences, the second half of the film utilises a slightly more dynamic shooting style, with more camera movement and additional point-of-view shots each time the troupe enters or leaves the city.

63 Lu Xun, *Selected Stories*, p. 60.

64 Cui Shuqin, 'Negotiating In-Between', p. 120.

65 Stephen Teo, 'Cinema with an Accent', in *Senses of Cinema*, available at <www.sensesofcinema.com/contents/01/15/zhangke_interview.html>

66 For several of the details surrounding this scene, I am indebted to assistant director Gu Zheng's essay 'Siji zhong de zhantai' ('Four Seasons on the Platform') in Lin Xudong, Zhang Yaxuan and Gu Zheng, *Jia Zhangke dianying: Zhantai*, p. 233.

67 See Xiaoping Lin, 'Jia Zhangke's Cinematic Trilogy', p. 203.

68 Berry, *Speaking in Images*, p. 204.

69 Lin Xudong, Zhang Yaxuan and Gu Zheng, *Jia Zhangke dianying*: Ren xiaoyao, p. 107.

70 Ibid., p. 120.

71 Jin Liu, 'The Rhetoric of Local Languages as the Marginal', p. 184.

72 See Liang Xiaosheng, *Jiusan duanxiang: Shei shi chouluo de zhongguoren* ('93 Randon Thoughts: Who is the Ugly Chinaman?') (Taiyuan: Shanxi gaoxiao lianhe chubanshe, 1994).

73 Collectively, these real-life news items that appear throughout the narrative also serve as temporal markers tracing the historical timeline against which the action plays out. The Hainan Incident, involving a US spy plane colliding with a Chinese jet over Chinese airspace, occurred on 1 April

2001, giving rise to large scale anti-American sentiment in China. The decision that Beijing would be the city to host the 2008 Olympic games was announced on 13 July 2001. And the five followers of Fulun Gong setting themselves aflame in Tiananmen Square occurred on 23 January 2001, although the news report featured is most likely from later that year.

74 Chuang Tzu, *The Complete Works of Chuang Tzu*, translated by Burton Watson (New York: Columbia University Press, 1968), p. 49. (Wades Giles romanisation has been replaced with *pinyin* in this excerpt.)

75 Tonglin Lu has offered an extended analysis of Qiaoqiao's wigs in the film. See 'Trapped Freedom and Localized Globalism', in Paul G. Pickowicz and Yingjin Zhang (eds), *From Underground to Independent: Alternative Film Culture in Contemporary China* (Lanham: Rowan & Littlefield, 2006), pp. 129–32.

76 Ibid., p. 135.

77 Lin Xudong, Zhang Yaxuan and Gu Zheng, *Jia Zhangke dianying: Ren xiaoyao*, p. 107.

78 McGrath, 'The Independent Cinema of Jia Zhangke', p. 105.

79 See Kevin Lee's profile of Jia in the online journal Senses of Cinema, available at <www.sensesofcinema.com/contents/directors/03/jia.html#14>

80 Tonglin Lu, 'Trapped Freedom and Localized Globalism', p. 137.

81 Berry, *Speaking in Images*, p. 205.

82 Lin Xudong, Zhang Yaxuan and Gu Zheng, *Jia Zhangke dianying: Ren xiaoyao*, p. 109.

83 Further conflating the possible intertextual connection between *Platform* and *Still Life* is the fact that while Sanming's character can possibly be interpreted as a recurring role, both Wang Hongwei and Zhao Tao also appear in *Still Life* in roles clearly different from Cui Mingliang and Yin Ruijuan from *Platform*.

84 See Xi Chuan's comments in the dialogue published in Ouyang Jianghe, *On the Edge*, p. 255.

85 *Breakin'* (aka *Breakdance The Movie*) was a popular 1984 film about the trails and tribulations of a group of urban breakdancers. The film was a major hit in China during the mid-1980s when it was released under the title, *Pili wu*. The film even inspired Fifth Generation director Tian Zhuangzhuang's *Rock Kids* (*Yaogun qingnian*).

86 After the success of his work with Jia Zhangke, Wang Hongwei has become increasingly in demand as an actor and was featured in Dai Sijie's production of his novel, *Balzac and the Little Chinese Seamstress* (2002).

87 Besides being an established cinematographer who has shot such features as Ann Hui's *Ordinary Heroes* (*Qianyan wanyu*) and William Kwok's *In the Dumps* (*Laji niantou*) Nelson Yu Lik Wai (1966–) is also an established director in his own right. His 1999 feature *Love Will Tear Us Apart* (*Tian shang renjian*) was an official selection at Cannes the year of its release, and is also playfully referenced in *Unknown Pleasures*.

Credits

Xiao Wu/Pickpocket
Hong Kong/China
1997

Presented by
Wang Hanbing
Producers
Li Kit-Ming (Li Jieming)
Jia Zhangke
Writer/Director
Jia Zhangke
Cinematography
Nelson Yu Lik Wai
(Yu Liwei)
Sound/Editing
Lin Xiaoling
Sound Mixer
Zhang Yang
Art Director
Liang Jingdong
First Assistant Director
Gu Zheng
Second Assistant
Director
Zhang Xi
Continuity
Luo Sha
Lighting
Sam Koa (Gu Yibin)
Camera Assistants
Guan Ying
Bill Chiu Chak Piu
(Zhao Zebiao)
Sound Assistant
Wei Xiaoyuan
Art Department
Lu Junwu
Liu Qiang
Production Manager
Wang Hongwei

Production Assistants
Jia Hao
Li Qiang
Jiao Wenhua
Xue Chunsheng
Lab Consultant
Xie Zhengyu
Production Stills
Wang Lei
Zhu Jiong (Zhu Qiong)

CAST
Wang Hongwei
Hao Hongjian
Zuo Baitao
Ma Jinrei
Liu Junying
Liang Yonghao
An Qunyan
Jiang Dongdong
Zhao Long
Wang Reiren (Wang
Ruiren)
Jinfeng Gao (Gao Jinfeng)
Li Renzhu (Li Runzhu)
Wu Juan
Ji Jinshu
Ren Zhaorui
Zhang Xiaohua
Zhang Deping
Qiao Yingfei
Wei Xiaoqin
Qiao Qiao
Zhao Genzhi

Zhantai/Platform
Hong Kong/China/
Japan
2000

Writer/Director
Jia Zhangke
Producers
Li Kit-Ming (Li Jieming)
Shozo Ichiyama
Executive Producer
Masayuki Mori
Co-producers
Joël Farges
Elise Jalladeau
Associate Producers
Chow Keung (Zhou
Qiang)
Nelson Yu Lik Wai (Yu
Liwei)
Production
Coordinator
Fumiko Osaka
Consultant
Lin Xudong
Literary Planner
Gu Zheng
Sound Director
Zhang Yang
Director of
Photography
Nelson Yu Lik Wai (Yu
Liwei)
Art Director
Qiu Sheng
Editor
Kong Jinlei
Composer
Yoshihiro Hanno

Assistant Directors
Gu Zheng
Zhang Xi
Tao Jun
Wang Yu
Gong Chun
Dai Yingying
Continuity
Luo Sha
Production Manager
Sheng Zhimin
Unit Manager
Li Runqiu
Local Production
Zhao Dengxin
Yi Jianwen
An Qunyan
Assistant Production Managers
Zhao Dengxin
Yin Jianwen
An Qunyan
Production Assistants
Shen Menglong
Jiao Wanji
Liang Yonghao
Li Xiaodong
Liang Wenqi
Hao Hongjian
Assistant Director of Photography
Yao Jianyun
Camera Assistant
Liu Shuhe
Lighting
Yao Jianyun
Sound Assistants
Yuan Hui
Xiao Baohua
Flute
Li Hongyun

Accordian
Wang Jian
Art Consultants
Liang Jingdong
Song Yongping
Assistant Art Director
Wang Zhigang
Costume Designers
Qi Lei
Zhao Xiafei
Costume Assistant
Zhang Jing
Make-up
Zheng Liwei
Dong Mei
Propmasters
An Qunyan
Yang Dawen
Jian Zheng Song (Jiang Jianxiong)
Tang Han Wing (Deng Hanrong)
Set Decorators
Yuan Minsheng
Wen Sheng
Wei Wen
Li Litian
Chen Sen
Zhang Jianping
Production Stills
Ricky Wong (Huang Dazhi)
Du Haibin
Kim Pai Jung (Jin Bizhen)
Making of Documentary
Kim Pai Jung (Jin Bizhen)
Chow Chi Sang (Zhou Zhisheng)
English Translation
Jeannie Wong (Huang Lizhen)

English Subtitles
Tony Rayns
Negative Cutter
Fong Hing Lun (Fang Qingling)
Lighting Assistants
Xie Hongjian
Gao Hujie
Si Guoli
Zhao Qinghai
Li Xunbo
Location Sound Assistant
Jiang Peng
Boom Operators
Yuan Hui
Xiao Baohua
Sound Engineer
Shen Jianqin
Engineers
Gary Sze
Chen Yuk Fung
Grips
Kong Yuping
Li Yan
Zhang Wei
Chow Chi Sang
Zhang Yongsheng
Gaffer
Yao Jianyun
Assistant Gaffers
Si Xuewen
Cao Ziping
Carpenters
Liang Yongfeng
Zhou Changshui
Laundry
Wen Ermei
Wang Huizhen

Costumers
Liang Xiaoxian
Huo Guihua

CAST
Wang Hongwei
Zhao Tao
Liang Jingdong
Yang Tianyi
Song Yongping
Wang Bo
Liu Juan
Liu E
Xi Chuan
Liang Yonghao
Li Mingzhu
Li Hongyun
Wen Xuefeng
San Lin
Xiangli Hongli
Sun Xiaojuan
He Runfu
Zhang Guihua
Lin Xudong
Hao Jun
Liang Anpeng
Han Sanming
Ren Huanlong
Yin Jianwen
Zheng Ping
Jiao Wanji
Gu Zheng
Du Weidong
Xu Weimin
Guo Yuxiang
Li Yu
Zhang Yaxin
Chen Shaojing
Chen Yushan

Ren Xiaoyao/Unknown Pleasures
Hong Kong/China/France
2002

Presented by
Wang Hanbing
Producers
Shozo Ichiyama
Li Kit-Ming (Li Jieming)
Executive Producers
Masayuki Mori
Hengameh Panahi
Paul Yi
Co-producer
Yuji Sadai
Associate Producers
Chow Keung (Zhou Qiang)
Nelson Yu Lik Wai (Yu Liwei)
Fumiko Osaka
Writer/Director
Jia Zhangke
Director of Photography
Nelson Yu Lik Wai (Yu Liwei)
Sound Design
Zhang Yang
Art Director
Liang Jingdong
Editor
Chow Keung (Zhou Qiang)
Literary Supervisor
Gu Zheng
First Assistant Director
Wang Yu

Second Assistant Director
Hou Mingjie
Third Assistant Director
Gu Zheng
Fourth Assistant Director
Dai Yingying
Continuity
Qi Jun
Production Manager
Li Zhujing
Production Secretary
Makoto Kakurai
Assistant Production Managers
Li Zhubin
Wang Limin
Li Yahui
Production Assistants
Liu Min
Song Juzhong
Assistant Cameraman
Liu Shuhe
Camera Assistant
Sun Yanchao
Gaffers
Si Xuewen
Si Guoli
Assistant Art Director
Cui Junjie
Wardrobe
Feng Yuyun
Make-up
Liu Huimin
Property Master
Deng Jinping
Assistant Sound Designer
Wu Jianqin

Boom Operator
Wu Jianxun
Sound Mix Engineer
Shen Jianqin
Sound Editor
Han Bing
**Post-production
Assistant**
Chow Chi Sang (Zhou Zhisheng)
Production Stills
Kim Pil Jung (Jin Bizhen)
Translator
Wang Weiqing
English Subtitles
Tony Rayns
Title Calligraphy
Wang Hanbing
Drivers
Song Juzhong
Shao Anguo
Pan Jingen
**Post-production
Supervisors**
Caroline Ghienne
Marc Moreaux

**Digital Video
Colourgrading**
Raymond Terrentin
Supervision
Philippe Reinaudo
Gerard Soirant
Coordination
Odile Beraud
Follow-up
Carole Vasseur

CAST
Zhao Tao
Qiaoqiao
Zhao Weiwei
Binbin
Wu Qiong
Xiao Ji
Li Zhubin
Qiao San
Zhou Qingfeng
Yuanyuan
Wang Hongwei
Xiao Wu
Bai Ru
Binbin's mother
Liu Xi'an
Xiao Ji's father

Xu Shulin
Sister Zhu
Ren Aijun
Hairdresser
Xiao Dao
Mr Ren
Ying Zi
Concubine
Wang Limin
Karaoke boss
Hou Mingjie
Karaoke customer
Song Juzhong
Chairman of the Estate Committee
Fu Hua
Nurse A
Zhang Shumin
Nurse B
Si Xuewen
First policeman
Liu Min
Second policeman
Jia Zhangke
Mr Ma
Liu Huimin
TV presenter

Bibliography

Ban Wang, 'Epic Narrative, Authenticity, and the Memory of Realism: Reflections on Jia Zhangke's *Platform*', in Ching Kwan Lee and Guobin Yang (eds), *Re-envisioning the Chinese Revolution: The Politics and Poetics of Collective Memories in Reform China* (Stanford: Stanford University Press, 2007), pp. 193–216.

Berry, Chris, 'Xiao Wu: Watching Time Go By', in Chris Berry (ed.), *Chinese Films in Focus II* (London: BFI, 2008).

Berry, Michael, 'Cultural Fallout', *Film Comment*, March/April 2003.

Berry, Michael, *Speaking in Images: Interviews with Contemporary Chinese Filmmakers* (New York: Columbia University Press, 2005).

Cao Kai, *Jilu yu shiyan: DV yingxiang qianshi (Documentary and Experimentation: A Prehistory of Digital Filmmaking)* (Beijing: Zhongguo renmin daxue chubanshe, 2005).

Cha Ling, *Lu Xun and the True Story of Ah Q (Lu Xun yu Ah Q zhengzhuan)* (Taipei: Siji chubanshe, 1981).

Chatterjee, Gayatri, Awāra (New Delhi: Penguin Books India, 2003).

Cheng Qingsong and Huang Ou, 'Jia Zhengke: Zai zhantai dengdai' ('Jia Zhangke: Waiting on the Platform), in *Wo de sheyingji bu sahuang: xianfeng dianying ren dangan – shengya 1961–1970 (My Camera Doesn't Lie)* (Beijing: Zhongguo youyi chubanshe, 2002), pp. 333–80.

Chuang Tzu, *The Complete Works of Chuang Tzu*, translated by Burton Watson (New York: Columbia University Press, 1968).

Cui Shuqin, 'Negotiating In-Between: On New-generation Filmmaking and Jia Zhangke's Films', *Modern Chinese Literature and Culture* vol. 18 no. 2, Autumn 2006, pp. 98–130.

Foster, Paul, *Ah Q Archaeology: Lu Xun, Ah Q Progeny and the National Character Discourse in Twentieth-Century China* (Lanham: Lexington Books, 2006).

Genette, Gerard, *Palimpsests* (Lincoln: University of Nebraska Press, 1997).

Hoberman, J., 'Please Watch Carefully: The Heart of the World', in *Chicago Reader*, available at <http://www.chicagoreader.com/movies/archives/2001/0102/010223.html>

Jia Zhangke, 'Wo de "zhangbei" Matian Shigaoxisi' ('My Eldership of Film' [sic]), *City Magazine*, April 2006.

Jiang Yuanlun and Shi Jian (eds), *Xianfeng, Duihua: Women yijing xuanze (Avant-Garde Dialogues: We Have Already Chosen)* (Guilin: Guangxi Normal University Press, 2004).

Jiang Yuanlun (eds), *Jinri xianfeng (Avant-Garde Today)* no. 12 (special issue on Jia Zhangke) (Tianjin: Tianjin shehui kexueyuan, 2002).

Jin Lin, 'The Rhetoric of Local Languages as the Marginal: Chinese Underground and Independent Films by Jia Zhangke and Others', *Modern Chinese Literature and Culture* vol. 18 no. 2, Autumn 2006, pp. 163–205.

Jones, Andrew F., *Like a Knife: Ideology and Genre in Contemporary Chinese Popular Music* (Ithaca: Cornell University East Asia Program, 1992).

Jones, Kent, 'Out of Time', *Film Comment* vol. 38 no. 5, 2002.

Kang Xingxuan and Chen Fang, 'I Believe in the Cultural Value of My Films' ('Wo xiangxin ziji de dianying wenhua jiazhi'), in *Ming Pao Monthly*, December 2006 pp. 70–5.

Kraicer, Shelly, 'Interview with Jia Zhangke', *Cineaction* no. 60, 2003.

Liang Xiaosheng, *Jiusan duanxiang: Shei shi chouluo de zhougguoren* ('93 Random Thoughts: Who is the Ugly Chinaman?') (Taiyuan: Shanxi gaoxiao lianhe chubanshe, 1994).

Li Xun, 'Zhongguo duli dianyingren' ('Chinese Independent Film-maker'), in Wang Shuo (ed.), *Dianying chufang:Dianying zai Zhongguo* (Celluloid Kitchen: Film in China) (Shanghai: Shanghai wenyi chubanshe, 2001), pp. 147–64.

Lin Xudong, Zhang Yaxuan and Gu Zheng, *The Films of Jia Zhangke:* Xiao Wu (Jia Zhangke Guxiang sanbuqu zhi Xiao Wu) (Beijing: Zhongguo mangwen chubanshe, 2003).

Lin Xudong, Zhang Yaxuan and Gu Zheng, *The Films of Jia Zhangke:* Platform (Jia Zhangke Guxiang sanbuqu zhi Zhantai) (Beijing: Zhongguo mangwen chubanshe, 2003).

Lin Xudong, Zhang Yaxuan and Gu Zheng, *The Films of Jia Zhangke:* Unknown Pleasures (Jia Zhangke Guxiang sanbuqu zhi Ren xiaoyao) (Beijing: Zhongguo mangwen chubanshe, 2003).

Liu, Jin, 'The Rhetoric of Local Languages as the Marginal: Chinese Underground and Independent Films by Jia Zhangke and Others', *Modern Chinese Literature and Culture* vol. 18 no. 2, Autumn 2006, pp. 163–205.

Lu, Tonglin, 'Trapped Freedom and Localized Globalism', in Paul G. Pickowicz and Yingjin Zhang (eds), *From Underground to Independent: Alternative Film Culture in Contemporary China* (Lanham: Rowan & Littlefield, 2006), pp. 123–41.

Lu Xun, *Selected Stories* (New York: W. W. Norton, 2003).

McGrath, Jason, 'The Independent Cinema of Jia Zhangke: From Postsocialist Realism to a Translational Aesthetic', in Zhang Zhen (ed.), *The Urban Generation: Chinese Cinema and Society at the Turn of the Twenty-first Century* (Durham: Duke University Press, 2007), pp. 81–114.

Ouyang Jianghe (ed.), *On the Edge: Chinese Independent Cinema* (Zhongguo duli dianying fangtanlu) (Oxford: Oxford University Press, 2007).

Rea, Dennis, *Live at the Forbidden City: Musical Encounter in China & Taiwan* (Lincoln, NE: iUniverse, 2007).

Stephen Teo, 'Cinema with an Accent', in *Senses of Cinema*, available at <http://www.sensesofcinema.com/contents/01/15/zhangke_interview.html>

Tonglin, Lu, 'Trapped Freedom and Localized Globalism', in Paul G. Pickowicz and Yingjin Zhang (eds), *From Underground to Independent: Alternative Film Culture in Contemporary China* (Lanham: Rowan & Littlefield, 2006).

Various authors, *Ming Pao Monthly*, December 2006 (Special Issue on Jia Zhangke).

Wu Wenguang (ed.), *Xianchang (Document)* 1 (2000) (special feature on Jia Zhangke's *Xiao Wu*) (Tianjin: Tianjin sheke, 2000).

Xiaoping Lin, 'Jia Zhangke's Cinematic Trilogy: A Journey across the Ruins of Post-Mao China', in Sheldon H. Lu and Emilie Yueh-yu Yeh (eds), *Chinese-Language Film: Historiography, Poetics, Politics* (Honolulu: University of Hawaii Press, 2005), pp. 186–209.

Yingjin Zhang, 'My Camera Doesn't Lie? Truth, Subjectivity, and Audience in Chinese Independent Film and Video', in Paul G. Pickowicz and Yingjin Zhang (eds), *From Underground to Independent: Alternative Film Culture in Contemporary China* (Lanham: Rowan & Littlefield, 2006), pp. 23–45.

Zhang Xianmin, *Invisible Images (Kanbujian de yingxiang)* (Shanghai: Shanghai Sanlian, 2004).